NATURALLY GOOD
David and Marlena Spieler
With a foreword by Juliette de Bäiradi Levy

FABER AND FABER
3 QUEEN SQUARE · LONDON

First published in 1974
by Faber and Faber Limited
3 Queen Square London WC1
Printed in Great Britain by
Whitstable Litho Straker Brothers Ltd

ISBN 0 571 10468 1

Foreword

I met David and Marlena Spieler in a village in Upper Galilee, Israel, where I have my vines and herbs. I had heard about them already from a group of young artists with whom they were staying and who had told me that they had been enjoying the most fantastic meals prepared by their visitors.

When I met the Spielers I was intrigued to find that they were travelling far and wide in search of food recipes, as I travel in search of herbs, and that they had written a book. I felt I'd met kindred spirits! As for the book: it was no ordinary collection of recipes. There was health there and the joy of good eating, with true originality in the way the recipes were being presented to the reader. Then, for very good measure, this was an illustrated food book, with Marlena's talented and rhythmical drawings to make the turning over of every page a curious and enjoyable experience.

The Spielers told me that soon they would be searching for a publisher for their book; I gave them the address of Faber and Faber, who have published most of my books, and I was of course very happy to hear a while later that Fabers shared my admiration for this truly original and interesting book. I hope that it proves to be a best-seller! It will certainly make for healthier, better and brighter eating.

Juliette de Baïracli Levy
Galilee, 1973

PREFACE

Writing _Naturally Good_ has been a very personal experience, as if collecting recipes and stories for a close friend. Here is how it all came about.

David began his culinary education while still a small child in the multi-national streets of a now-disappeared old New York. The journey from the street to his apartment was punctuated with aromas reminiscent of the Ukraine, Poland, Malta, Puerto Rico, Syria, and the American deep south. Sometimes it took forever to reach home! Chinatown and "Little Italy" were just around the corner, one or the other usually celebrating a holiday or feast replete with special foods. It was the perfect place to sample the flavors of a simmering "melting pot".

Marlena spent her early years in California where fresh produce, especially salads, is always in season. Mexican specialities, spicy and pungent, Russian-Jewish family dishes as well as exotic Chinese foods helped form her tastes.

Together we shared the joys of food preparation and, of course, eating. Our table was always filled with friends eager to taste and enjoy whatever new creation we could offer. David was studying restaurant management, Marlena studying art. These lessons were all invaluable to us in creating this book and, we hope, in future projects.

Our search for knowledge of foods and the way people eat took us to many places; to small regional areas of foreign lands, where we could taste dishes at their most authentic, and to many of

...the communes that dot the U.S.A. where we prepared feasts with the limited foods available. We began to learn the sources of food: how to grow a garden, raise chickens, milk goats and to forage for wild things, herbs and berries especially.

On our travels we found that "food conversation" is a great way to meet people. If we knew only three words in a language the first two were usually national dishes we were wanting to try (the third was the word for water-closet). When natives saw our interest in their beloved foods, they would offer advice on how "Mother used to make it......" or, grabbing us by the arms, would usher us to the shop "that has the best spices on the island."

The notes we amassed during these years of pleasurable wandering were the basis of this book. While in Israel we met Juliette de Baïracli Levy who inspired us with her wondrous knowledge of herbs and whose encouragement enabled us to reach a better understanding of what we were putting together. Shortly thereafter we found ourselves in London at the door of Faber and Faber, our arms laden with manuscript and homemade rum babas.

None of this book would have been possible without the help, companionship and ideas of so many people along the way. To Jude and Mike Gold, whose home in London was opened to us, to Richard and Linda for visions of Moroccan feasts, to Sonny and Rina who faithfully tested recipes and to Danny Glaser, and our many friends in Rosh Pinna, Israel, we are very grateful.

8

A special thanks to Jeanie Darlington for her tomato-herb soup which was first printed in the now defunct "San Francisco Express Times", to Jill Miller for the recipe for Vietnamese soup-salad from her book VIETNAMESE COOKERY, Charles Tuttle, publishers, to Ed Rosenfeld for his "Rosenfeld's Chinese duck", and to Joyce Stubbs for "filo dough" from her excellent book The Home Book of Greek Cookery, Faber and Faber publishers.

We are indebted to Caroline Hartnell whose Transatlantic editing got the book together and especially to everyone at Faber and Faber.

This book is dedicated to Heidi, Gretchen, and Sasha who sometimes like this or maybe don't like that, but always like our cooking, to Bachi for her inspiration and help and to the memory of Helen Spieler.

May Naturally Good bring to you as much joy reading and creating from it as it has brought us writing it.

David and Marlena Spieler

AUTHORS' NOTE

For reasons of taste and/or economy any of the stews can be adjusted to your own needs by decreasing the amount of meat and adding more vegetable. Another favorite way of enjoying the vegetable course is simply to steam it. You'll be pleasantly surprised at how alive the food will taste: barely tender, the color will be bright, the texture firm, the flavor wholesomely rich. One can buy a gadget that fits well into almost any sized pot. It is inexpensive and available in health food stores and culinary food shops. It's good also, for steaming grape leaves, making steamed bread and warming leftovers, especially rice.

About utensils, we are informal, relaxed cooks. If a certain pot is not available we make do. One must! What is important is the substance that the pots are made of. In general we are very fond of cast iron for sautéing, roasting and frying. It conducts the heat well, is inexpensive and incredibly durable. Stainless steel and enamel are excellent for cooking liquids, the latter less expensive but not lasting terribly well. A few good knives — a french knife, a boning knife (made from steel — not stainless steel which is too difficult to sharpen), are important.

The most important ingredient in a successful dish is you! Enjoy your food. Eat slowly, savoring the moment. Never eat too fast or too much. Take a few sips of wine or juice, exchange words and ideas with family or companions. A peaceful and warm mealtime can nourish not only your body, but your soul.

What we have tried to do here is present a collection of interesting and unusual foods, which are easy and rewarding to prepare. We've not made an attempt to compile a basic primer; instead, a simple, joyful book of recipes and ideas.

Though we're very interested in healthful eating we've made no recommendations as to diets. We personally believe that one should eat a well-balanced diet of the freshest vegetables, herbs, fruits, meats, seafoods, eggs, grains and dairy products, and generally try to avoid refined flour, sugar, greasy fried dishes and overcooked foods. However, everybody is different and while one of us thrives on a diet of roasts, ale and other hearty foods, someone else could not eat such a diet and prefers steamed fish with sautéed vegetables (we are happiest with some of each). The important thing is to listen to your body: it will tell you of its needs.

You may notice the large collection of salad recipes and the small number for cooked vegetables. This is because many of the main dishes, soups, cheese and egg dishes contain substantial amounts of vegetables. These also tend to be quite rich and we prefer them with the contrast of a cold salad.

CONTENTS

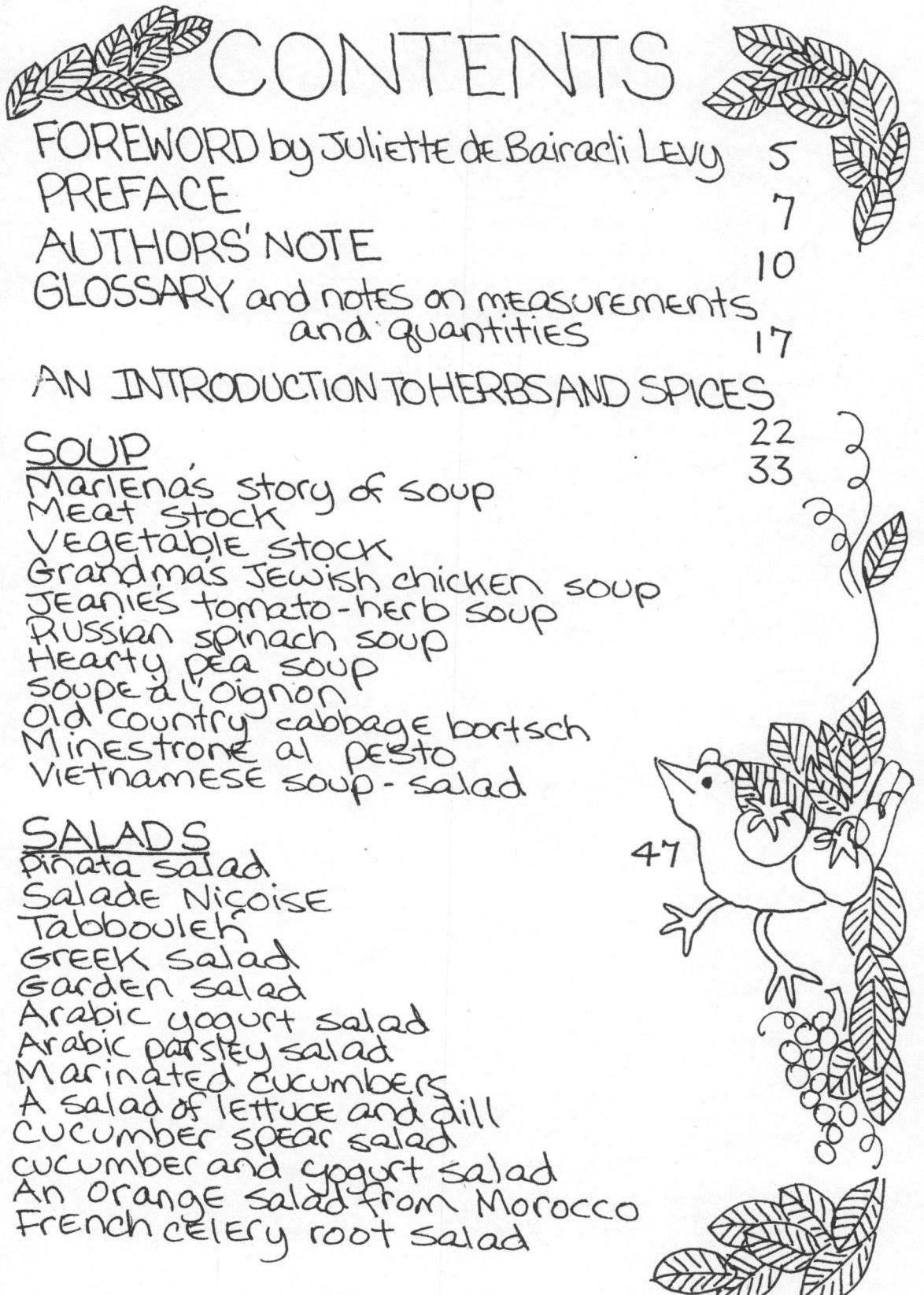

14

Roast chicken tarragon
Chicken paprikash
Chicken Lily
Pastilla (Bestella)
Rosenfeld's Chinese duck
Fondue bourguignonne
Leg of lamb, desert tribe style
Roasted lamb shanks
Lamb and vegetables
A stew of roots and lamb
Moroccan lamb and eggplant
Moussaka
Jaffa Gate spinach
Sautéed liver
Sweetbreads Italian style
Choucroute garnie

SAUCES   125
Tahina and variations
Guacamole
Salsa cruda
Pesto alla genovese
Saté sauce
Mom's Barbeque sauce
Greek lemon sauce
Tomato sauce
Rémoulade sauce
Dilled sour cream
Mustard-mayonnaise
Sauce au crème

BREADS AND SANDWICHES 137
Basic wheat bread
Onion bread
Sopiapillas
Steamed bread
The American burger
Guadalajara Sandwich
Avocado Sandwiches

GLOSSARY

<u>buckwheat noodles</u> - thin noodles made from buckwheat flour. Available in Oriental shops as Japanese 'soba' or sometimes in health food stores. Thin whole wheat spaghetti may be substituted.

<u>bulgar wheat</u> - the whole grain of the wheat, partially milled and steamed, then dried. Sometimes called "pilaff" (not to be confused with rice pilaff). Find bulgar wheat at health food or Middle Eastern speciality shops.

<u>cheehou</u> - a sweet and spicy Chinese sauce based on fermented bean paste. Available in tins from Chinese food shops.

<u>Chorizo</u> - a highly spiced pork sausage favored among the Basques, the Spanish and the Mexicans.

<u>Corn chips</u> are an American speciality: small flat rectangles or triangles of finely ground corn meal, deep fried and crispy.

<u>Couscous</u> - a pellet-shaped tiny pasta-like grain of wheat, popular in North Africa. Buy in Middle Eastern speciality shops.

<u>Fetta cheese</u> - a salty white semi-crumbly ewe cheese from Greece. Sold in Middle Eastern food shops.

<u>fontina</u> - a semi-soft fairly mild cheese from Italy.

<u>hoisin</u> - another prepared Chinese sauce based on fermented beans.

kasha- the whole grain of the buckwheat, very slightly milled. Cooked as a porridge and eaten with meats or fowl or sweetened and accompanied with milk for breakfast. Available in health food stores.

liquid smoke- the distilled liquid from burning hickory wood. Use sparingly. If not available substitute a smoky flavored nutritional yeast or eliminate altogether.

look fun- dried rice noodles. Buy at Chinese food stores.

Monteray jack- a semi-soft cheese made in the U.S.A.

mozzarella cheese- a mild cheese from Italy, excellent for melting. The "pizza" cheese.

muenster- a semi-soft cheese from Germany.

nuoc mam is also called fish sauce or fish gravy. Used in Vietnamese and Chinese cookery. Find in Oriental food stores.

nutritional yeast- a brownish-colored powder which is an excellent source of the B vitamins, trace minerals and protein. Available at health food stores, nutritional yeast is excellent for fortifying foods.

orange flower water- a flavoring liquid distilled from orange blossoms. Used especially in Middle Eastern sweets.

raw sugar- partially refined sugar still retaining a good percentage of its molasses. Purchase in health food stores.

ricotta cheese- a smooth, light, low-fat

cheese from Italy. If ricotta is not available, sieved cottage cheese may be substituted.

rose water- similar to orange flower water, only distilled from the petals of roses. Find in Indian food stores.

sesame oil is the oil extracted from toasted sesame seeds. Used as flavoring in Chinese cookery.

shrimp, dried- tiny, dry salty shrimps. Find in Chinese food stores.

tortillas are the flat pancake-like cornbread that is the staple of Mexico.

vermicelli - very thin worm-like strands of spaghetti.

wheatgerm - the most nutritious part of the whole wheat grain, so often removed in milling. An excellent source of vitamin E and B complex. Find wheatgerm in health food stores and sprinkle over cereals, yogurt or ice cream, or include in baking breads and pastries.

yogurt cheese - a fresh, tart, creamy cheese made from suspending yogurt in a bag of cheesecloth for several days to extract the liquid.

MEASUREMENTS

WE have used the American cup, which has a capacity of 8 fluid ounces, as the unit of measurement throughout the book, and have given measurements in pounds and ounces only where the cup measurement would be inconvenient. For instance, we have given quantities of meat in pounds, as it would be impossible to buy it otherwise, but if a recipe uses scraps of leftover meat it is much easier to measure in cups. The same of course applies with cheese, vegetables, etc., but all dry ingredients and liquids are always measured in cups (or tablespoons or teaspoons, of course, when very small quantities are involved).

QUANTITIES

We have not always said exactly how many people each recipe will serve. We have done this for all main dish recipes, including the cheese and egg dishes and the pasta and grain dishes, for which quantities are especially hard to guess: it is impossible to tell how much an unknown sort of grain will expand in cooking.

On the other hand, one might have soup as part of a meal or as a meal in itself, and it is always quite easy to judge how much a recipe will make by the amount of liquid used, so we have not said how many people a soup recipe will serve. Similarly with a salad, which can be a starter, an accompaniment to a main course or a complete meal. And with sweet things appetites vary so enormously that it would be impossible to say how many people a pastry would serve!

A GENERAL INTRODUCTION TO HERBS and SPICES

<u>AniSEED</u> has a licorice-like flavor. It is the main flavoring ingredient for many liquors including ouzo, pernod, and arak and is also used in some bakery products. The Chinese use an unusual form of anise, star anise, whose seeds are enclosed in a largish star-shaped pod.

<u>Allspice</u> is not a combination of spices, as it sounds, but a small, brown, pepper-like berry with the aroma and flavor of cinnamon, clove, nutmeg and juniper. Use in sweet bakery goods, liver patés, Arabic style meat and vegetable stews, and tabbouléh.

<u>Basil</u> originated in India, where it is considered sacred and consequently is not often used. It is now enjoyed a great deal in southern French and Italian cookery. There are 2 varieties, purple and green, but the green is more commonly dried for culinary use because of its richer, sweeter aroma. Use fresh in pesto sauce, chopped and sprinkled onto salads or tomato soup. Use dried in tomato sauces, in boeuf bourguignome and as a combination with nutmeg in boeuf stroganoff.

<u>Bay leaves</u> grow on the laurel bay tree. They are especially good in tomato, lentil or split pea dishes, soups, and meat and vegetable stews.

<u>Camomile</u> often grows wild. It makes a wonderfully calming tea (especially to an upset stomach). So calming in fact to the whole body that the Italians believe a woman wishing for a night of rest has only to brew her husband a cup of camomile tea and he will not become sexually aroused. The well-strained tea is also an excellent hair rinse for blondes.

<u>Caraway seed</u> is what makes rye bread taste like rye bread. It's used in eastern European dishes such as sauerkraut and noodle or pork dishes.

<u>Cardamon</u> is a 3-sided pod containing small dark fragrant seeds. It should be bought in the pod and powdered only as required. It is used in Arabic cookery in such dishes as meat balls, spinach and chick peas or in Arabic coffee. It's especially good in such sweets as creamy tapioca pudding or Indian carrot halva. The Swedish use cardamon a great deal in their sweet pastries and breads.

<u>Cayenne pepper</u> is the small fiery red hot chilli peppers ground to a fine powder. Use in Mexican, Indian or North African dishes, or <u>very discreetly</u> in buttery bland sauces such as hollandaise.

<u>Celery seed</u> is a tiny distinctive-tasting seed, used in pickles, in soups, and on top of breads. It is not only celery seeds that are tasty, for every part of this plant has a culinary use. <u>Celery root</u> makes a good stock for soup, especially a lentil or mushroom and barley soup. Raw, it makes an unusual salad. The stem of the plant, <u>celery</u>, is crisp, fresh-tasting and very low in calories. It is eaten raw, cooked, marinated, diced, chopped, whole and sliced. Good in salads and soups. <u>Celery leaves</u> are used as a herb for flavoring soups, stews, and meat or fish dishes.

CHERVIL is a delicate, lacy-leafed biennial herb, one of the fines herbes of French cookery (the others are tarragon, chives and parsley). It is used in salads, soups, bean dishes and omelettes. A book on French cookery will yield many recipes for using chervil.

Chilli peppers (fresh or dried) are often used for spicing a dish. There are many varieties available, with varying degrees of hotness and slightly different flavors. Chillies are used a great deal in North African, Indian, Chinese, Mexican and Latin American cookery.

Chilli powder is a spice and herb mixture from the south-west United States. It's a combination of cumin, paprika, oregano and cayenne, occasionally containing such additions as cinnamon, cloves, and powdered garlic. It is the main seasoning for chilli con carne (chilli and meat and often beans) and for Tamale pie (a concoction of cornmeal, minced beef, tomatoes and corn), another speciality of the area.

Chives are a delicate member of the onion family. They grow in thin green shoots from a single clump and have lavender-colored blossom. Chop chives fresh and add to scrambled eggs or cottage cheese, or on top of potato soup.

Cinnamon is the bark from a tree that originated in Ceylon. Cinnamon is sold rolled up, scroll-like, and called "cinnamon sticks", or powdered. Use the stick as a stir for hot tea, coffee or chocolate. Brew with mulled wine or punch, and add to fruit and meat stews, Moroccan style. As a powder, cinnamon is good in tomato sauce, especially if raisins, lemon juice and honey are added to make a sweet and sour sauce. Sprinkle cinnamon and sugar on buttered toast and broil (grill) for a minute. Voilà: cinnamon toast! A happy treat for children at breakfast.

CLOVES are the tiny nail-shaped buds of the clove tree, used in curries and stewed fruits, especially apple. Good in marinades, pickles, glazed hams and minced meat preparations. Ground (powdered) cloves are used in sweets and bakery products. The oil extracted from cloves has various medicinal uses and is especially good dabbed sparingly and gently around an aching tooth.

Coriander, also known as Chinese parsley or Mexican cilantro or Arabic cousbarrah, is the herb grown from the coriander seed. It has a pungent, almost unpleasant odor and taste at first, but its flavor is so unique that one usually grows fond of it. It is prominent in much Mexican, North African, Indian and Middle Eastern cookery. It is simple and quick to grow. We have a great affection for this herb.

Coriander seed has a pleasant, somewhat sweet aroma. It is used as a curry seasoning, with fruit salad and in honey cakes. It's the primary spice in the all-American frankfurter. Coriander is one of the earliest herbs known to man (it's mentioned in Exodus of the Bible).

Cumin, ground, is the main ingredient in curry mixtures and in many North African, Mexican and Middle Eastern dishes. It's excellent with lamb, beans, yogurt or eggplant. In Holland and Denmark whole cumin seeds are used to flavor cheeses and breads as well as the liquors, aquavit and schnapps.

Dill, small, flat seeds or a long-stemmed feathery-leafed plant: both are used in potato dishes, marinated cucumbers, and with sour cream as a sauce. Probably best known for its combination with cucumbers in dill pickles.

25

Fennel has seeds that look very much like aniseed but larger and with a milder flavor. The plant itself is delightful. Its appearance is rather like squat celery with feathery leaves and its taste is mildly licorice-like. It can be cooked quickly and served with butter or tomato sauce, or eaten our favorite way: a simple salad of raw sliced fennel dressed with a fruity olive oil and lemon juice.

Fenugreek are little, hard, flattish, ochre-colored seeds, to which many medicinal qualities are attributed. Use as a pleasant tea or let the seeds sprout and eat them raw in salads, sandwiches, etc. As a culinary spice fenugreek figures prominently in Indian, Middle Eastern and Yemen cookery. The green herb which grows from these seeds is called methi and is eaten in India as greens.

Filé is the spice mixture that gives gumbo its gumbo-y taste. A creole speciality from the south-east United States, it is made from sassafras leaves, thyme and a pinch of either allspice, coriander and/or sage. Good in okra dishes, seafood or chicken gumbo, jambalaya. The root from the sassafras tree makes a delightful tea, tasting somewhat like root beer.

Garlic — Like the onion, garlic is a member of the Lily family. It has very strong anti-bacterial properties: squeeze a little garlic onto a nasty pimple; it should draw out the poison and dry the sore up. Many people claim that eating raw garlic every day keeps them from intestinal problems (we do this before a journey to a foreign country). During epidemics mothers used to give their children little packets of garlic to be worn around their necks. This doubled as an agent to ward off the evil spirits.

<u>Garlic</u> (continued) - Some people say that garlic is an aphrodisiac (Marlena thinks it smells sexy), and everyone <u>knows</u> that garlic wards off vampires.

As a culinary ingredient it is used in southern France, Italy, Greece, Mexico, India, Arabia, the Far East, Eastern Europe — indeed almost everywhere in the world. Use raw (minced or crushed) in salad dressings, marinades, herbed butters, tomato salads. Cook garlic with zucchini (courgettes), eggplant (aubergine), peppers, tomatoes, spinach, potatoes and almost any other vegetable. For those true afficionados here is a dish from Provence: Rub the outside of a chicken with crushed garlic and butter. Place in a pan to be roasted. Into its cavity put 25-40 (!) cloves of garlic, whole and peeled. Roast very slowly until golden brown. The long slow cooking tames the garlic's pungency and reduces it to a perfumed purée at the bottom of the pan. A delightful gravy for the chicken.

There are several sauces whose main flavoring ingredient is garlic, most notably the French aïoli and the Greek skortalia, both mayonnaise-type sauces eaten with boiled or fried fish and vegetables.

<u>Ginger</u> is a strange shaped bulbous root with a distinctive, pungent flavor. Ginger is used fresh, preserved in sugar syrup or dried and powdered. Used in Chinese, North African, and southern Italian cookery, as well as in gingerbread and curry powder. Ginger is good in certain marinades and has an affinity for duck.

<u>Horseradish</u>: This plant has huge roots which grow into the earth a good 3 or 4 feet. These roots have a very sharp, "hot" taste and make an excellent condiment. Simply grate a little horseradish root into a small amount of vinegar or lemon juice. Wonderful when added to sour cream as a sauce for meat, or mix the horseradish with a little beet juice and sugar for the traditional accompaniment to the Jewish dish, gefilte fish.

27

Juniper berries are the flavoring ingredient of gin. Juniper is good with meats, marinades, choucroute garnie, game birds and patés.

Lavender has fragrant little buds which when dried make lovely sachets. These are laid among the linen and clothes to perfume them. This herb has occasional culinary usage. A small amount of lavender is used in the North African spice mixture raz al hanout, as well as in a French Provençal spice mixture (along with basil, nutmeg, rosemary, thyme, cloves, bay leaf, coriander seed, savory and white pepper) used to season roast meats.

Mace and Nutmeg — Mace is the outer husk of the nutmeg fruit. Both have a sweet spicy aroma and are good in fruit dishes, curries and eggnogs. Nutmeg is especially good grated into cream sauces and spinach dishes, but remember, it's very strong and should be used sparingly.

Marjoram has a sweet herby flavor similar to oregano. Good fresh or dried in tomato dishes and meat stews and sprinkled atop fresh tomato soup.

Mint — There is a whole family of mints: spearmint, peppermint, applemint, pineapple mint, and many more. Some have a sweeter aroma, some a more peppery one. Catmint, otherwise known as catnip, intoxicates cats: they roll about in it, writhing with pleasure. For us humans, it makes a pleasant tea. Use mint fresh or dried in fruit salad, green salad, cooked peas, stuffed vine leaves, or tabbouleh. Oil of mint can be used very, very sparingly as a flavoring in sweets, or a tiny drop of the essential oil can be added to a cup or so of pure salad oil (no preservatives!) to make a soothing lubricant good for massages (other essential oils with mild fragrances are good too).

Mustard - The 2 most common mustard seeds are the yellow and black ones. From these seeds are prepared many different types of mustard: Chinese hot, American bland, French champagne-flavored, English sharp or Russian sweet. The seeds can be used whole as a seasoning in pickles, curries, Indian rice dishes, and eggplant and yogurt dishes. The yellow flowering plants that cover the countryside in early spring are usually wild mustard. The greens taste somewhat like sharp broccoli and can be eaten in salads, omelettes and minestrone soup.

Oregano is a fragrant green herb favored in Italy, Mexico, Greece, and Spain. Use in tomato sauce or soup, in moussaka, or sprinkled on top of a Greek salad.

Paprika is ground from sweet red peppers. Spanish and Greek paprika tends to be more spicy, while Hungarian paprika is richer and sweeter. Paprika is the main flavoring of Goulash, paprikash and other Hungarian specialties. Sprinkle a little on meat, fish or chicken while roasting or sautéing to give a richer, browner color.

Parsley - There are 2 main varieties of this herb, flat leaf or Italian parsley and the curly parsley common to our markets. Rumor has it that parsley stems are an aphrodisiac. Whether or not this is true, parsley does contain many vitamins and has a purifying effect on the blood. Parsley can be used with meat, vegetables, salads and egg dishes. Top sliced tomatoes with chopped parsley and dribble over it with olive oil. Try sprinkling chopped parsley over grilled fish, sautéed liver, or boiled potatoes.

ROSEMARY loves the sun and once planted will grow almost forever. It has long spiky green branches that blossom with lavender or blue-colored flowers. Rosemary is a common ingredient in many hair preparations; a rinse of strained rosemary tea after shampooing is refreshing and beneficial, especially for brunettes. As a culinary ingredient, rosemary is pleasant with tomato dishes, chopped fresh into a green salad, roasted with lamb, whipped into creamed potatoes, or coating a chunk of cream cheese (which is then left overnight to ripen).

Saffron is the delicate red-colored stigmas of the autumn crocus. It takes 225,000 flowers to make 1 lb. of saffron—hence it is very expensive. Saffron is potent and used in small quantities. It gives a gentle yellow coloring to whatever it's cooked with, as well as a delicate and distinctive aroma. Dishes that use saffron are: paella, bouillabaisse, Italian risottos, North African couscous and stews, Indian curries and rice dishes.

Sage—There are many varieties of this herb, which is usually greyish green in color. In Greece the cafes exude the pungent smell of tea brewed from sage leaves. Sage is used to flavor sausages, chowders, and Christmas day stuffings. In Italy fresh sage leaves are placed on top of a piece of mild veal, a piece of salty prosciutto ham on top of that, then it's all sautéed in butter. This is called saltimbocca (jumps into the mouth!) alla Romana.

Savory, winter and summer—The winter variety of this herb is stronger and used in stews, meat loaves, etc. The summer variety is more delicate and lovely in salads and green bean or tomato dishes.

<u>Sumac</u> is a sour red berry that is ground and used as a spice in the Middle East. It is an ingredient in za'atar (see thyme), a seasoning in spinach-stuffed filo dough pastries, and occasionally an ingredient in a marinade for grilled chicken.

<u>Tarragon</u> is another of our favorite herbs. Delightful with chicken, fish, lamb chops or sweetbreads. As well as being dried, this herb is preserved well by placing the sprigs into a bottle of wine vinegar. This also perfumes the vinegar for lovely salad dressings.

<u>Thyme</u> — This herb also grows in many varieties. There is lemon thyme, named for its lemony fragrance, or silver thyme, named for its silver-colored leaves, and creeping thyme, which grows low and close to the ground giving the appearance of creeping. Thyme is good with veal, pork, fish and tomatoes. Mixed with sassafras leaves it is the mixture called filé gumbo. Mixed with roasted sesame seeds, sumac, salt and a little cumin, it is the Arabic mixture called za'atar, which is eaten with doughy Arabic bread, yogurt cheese* and fragrant olive oil as an everyday breakfast. A pinch of thyme is excellent added to fish stock or soup or to a roast duck.

<u>Tumeric</u> is a tuber which looks very much like a smaller, skinnier ginger root. However, its coloring and flavor are very distinctive. It could be called the poor man's saffron, in that it colors food cooked with it a warm yellow. Its taste, however, is stronger and warmer than that of saffron and a little bitter. It is much used in Indian, North African and Yemen cooking and is used in pickles and mustards.

31

~SOUP~

Is there anything so comforting or so diversified as soup? A thin, golden broth with threadlike drops. of egg; a purée of légumes so thick and hearty, boasting chunks of bacon; a rich consommé, permeated with the taste and aroma of sautéed onions and enriched with a dash of strong sherry; or even a cool, creamy liquid, redolent of cherries, cream and red wine.

Marlena's Story of Soup

"To me, soupmaking was the key to the whole of cookery. Somehow I'd never cooked, and after we'd been together a while, David asked to be prepared something. I'd been content until then eating David's lovely creations. His request threw me into a panic! ME, cook? I did not know where to begin and cookbooks were completely unknown to me.

"Salvation came in the form of a memory: every week my grandmother prepared chicken soup. Perhaps my first memory of life is of sipping this rich broth, with alphabet noodles or sometimes kasha*(buckwheat groats). From this childhood picture I drew up a recipe: chicken, onions, carrots, celery and parsley, remembering my grandmother's admonition:'Always a chicken foot.'

"Into the pot it all went, simmering beautifully all afternoon. The aroma filled the house. The children came in from playing commenting on how nice the kitchen smelled and 'Gee-what's for dinner?'

"In awe at having created such magic, I ladled the steamy liquid into bowls, marveling all the while. David said 'You are a good cook' the children said 'More soup!' and I savored the sweetness of a first accomplishment."

The most important ingredient for soup
is the liquid. Homemade stocks make the
best soups!

MEAT STOCK

Anything, within reason of course, can go
into a stockpot: leftover bones from last night's
supper, vegetable parings. A freezer is a good
tool to utilize: you can freeze and store wilted
vegetables, bones and meat trimmings, saving
them all up for soup day.

3 lb beef bones   3 lb lamb neck
2 turnips   } diced
4-5 carrots   2 onions, cut up

Other ingredients such as chicken parts,
duck bones and/or veal bones may be added as
well as any vegetable - celery root, lettuce, parsnip,
celery - you wish.

For a light stock simply place the meat,
bones and vegetables in a large pot, add several
bay leaves, peppercorns and several tbsp. herb
vinegar. For a darker, browner stock, sauté the
vegetables, meat and bones first, adding ½ - 1 tsp.
of raw sugar. Then place it all in the pot with
the water and flavorings.

Bring to the boil, then reduce the heat and
simmer, covered, for 3-4 hours, or until it tastes
rich enough.

Your house will smell beautiful.

Skim off the excess fat; a simple way is to
chill the whole pot of soup. The fat will solidify and
can be lifted off.

Heat the broth and strain before serving
or using in another dish.

Serve the broth as a first course, garnished
with a wedge of lemon or lime or enriched with
some small soup pastas or meat filled ravioli.

35

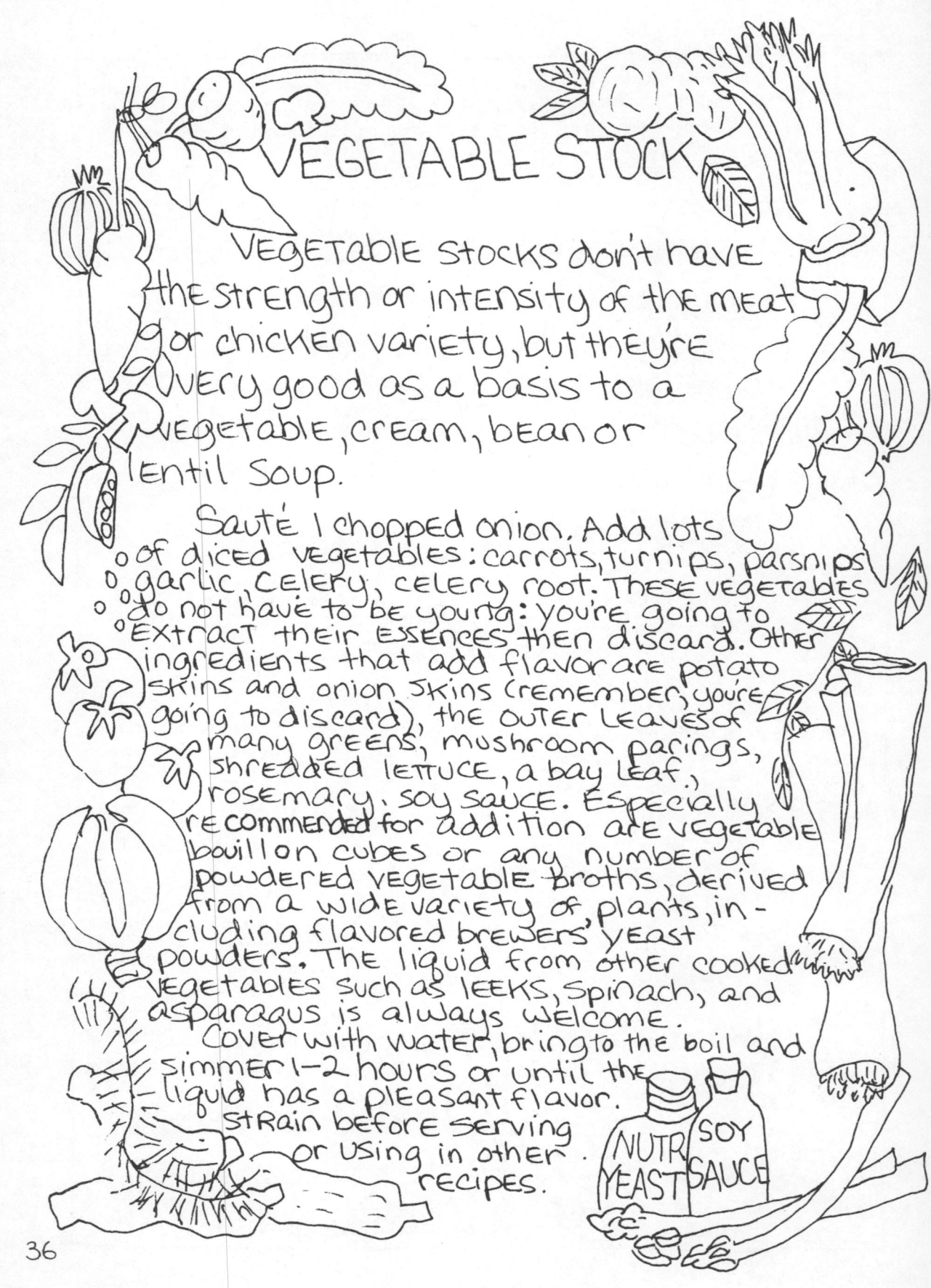

VEGETABLE STOCK

VEGETABLE stocks don't have the strength or intensity of the meat or chicken variety, but they're very good as a basis to a vegetable, cream, bean or lentil soup.

Sauté 1 chopped onion. Add lots of diced vegetables: carrots, turnips, parsnips garlic, celery, celery root. These vegetables do not have to be young: you're going to extract their essences then discard. Other ingredients that add flavor are potato skins and onion skins (remember, you're going to discard), the outer leaves of many greens, mushroom parings, shredded lettuce, a bay leaf, rosemary, soy sauce. Especially recommended for addition are vegetable bouillon cubes or any number of powdered vegetable broths, derived from a wide variety of plants, including flavored brewers' yeast powders. The liquid from other cooked vegetables such as leeks, spinach, and asparagus is always welcome.

Cover with water, bring to the boil and simmer 1-2 hours or until the liquid has a pleasant flavor. Strain before serving or using in other recipes.

NUTR YEAST   SOY SAUCE

GRANDMA'S JEWISH CHICKEN SOUP

1 chicken, jointed (including heart, liver, etc.)
1 or 2 cleaned chicken feet (optional)
several sprigs parsley
pinch of dill weed and dillseed
1 parsnip, sliced

6 carrots, sliced
1 quartered onion
3 stalks celery, sliced
salt and pepper, to taste

Place all this in a large pot and cover with cold water. Bring to the boil and simmer, covered, for several hours (3, at least). When it tastes rich and chickeny it's ready.

Chill, then spoon off excess fat from the top, and discard heart, gizzards, feet, etc.

Reheat and serve in bowls a little bit of the vegetables, a piece of chicken, some cooked noodles, rice or KASHA* (Buckwheat groats).

Any leftover soup may be strained and used later in other soups and dishes.

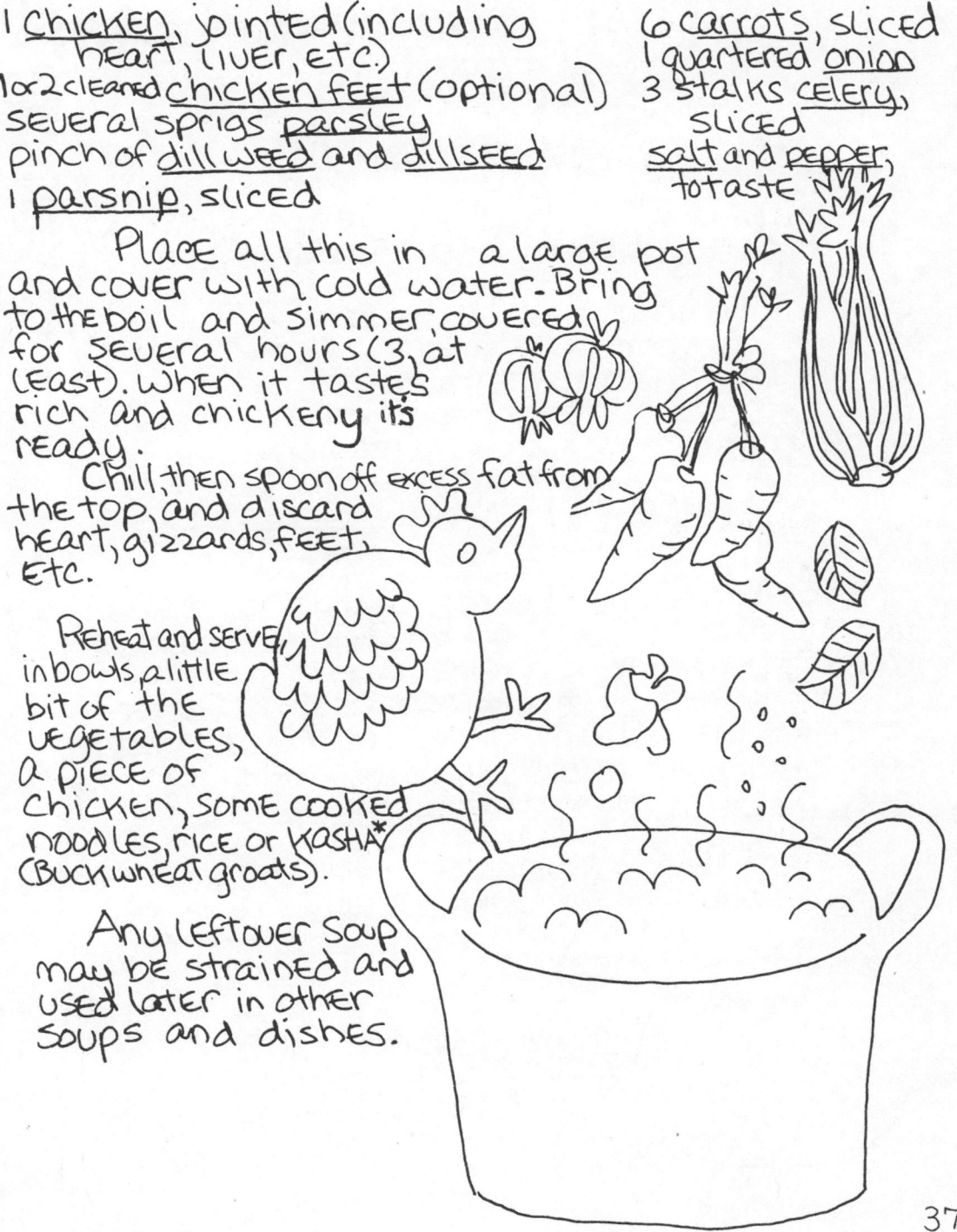

JEANIE'S TOMATO-HERB SOUP

Especially good made from vine-ripened richly red tomatoes!

Sauté in butter 'til limp 1 medium onion, chopped, and 2 or 3 cloves garlic. Then add 15-20 medium tomatoes, coarsely chopped, and continue cooking a few minutes longer.

Add approx. 4 cups chicken stock and cook 20 minutes.

Now to purée the mixture: either blend it in several batches in an electric blender, or mash it through a sieve (choose the latter to rid the soup of the tomato skins). Return soup to the pot and add 2 cups milk, salt and pepper to taste, and lots of fresh chopped parsley, basil and/or marjoram.

Heat through and serve garnished with a spoonful of sour cream and a sprinkling of parsley and herbs.

RUSSIAN SPINACH SOUP

On cold foggy days we often head toward San Francisco's Russian neighborhood. There we find a steamy café and amidst the chatter of Russian we warm ourselves with a hearty soup.

1 lb. raw <u>spinach</u>, washed & trimmed
1 <u>carrot</u>, finely chopped
4 cups <u>chicken stock</u>
1 medium/small <u>celery root</u>
pinch <u>dillweed</u>

1 <u>onion</u>
1 small <u>potato</u>
1 small <u>turnip</u>
1 small <u>parsnip</u>

Cut the turnip, parsnip, celery root, onion, and potato into ½-¾ inch chunks.

Place all ingredients in soup pot, including chicken stock and dillweed and bring soup to the boil. Then turn heat to low and simmer 25-30 minutes.

Serve garnished with <u>lemon wedges</u>, <u>hard-cooked egg slices</u>, <u>sour cream</u> and <u>parsley</u>.

39

HEARTY PEA SOUP

This soup is high in the B vitamins. IT is also tasty, fragrant and filling and excellent on a cold chilly day.

1. Sauté: several pieces streaky bacon, 1 chopped onion, 1 chopped carrot, 1 diced celery root, 2 bay leaves, 1 tsp. ground cumin, ½-1 tsp. sage. Remove mixture and place in soup pot.

2. Sauté: ⅓-½ lb. pork (meat and bones) and 1 ham hock or several spicy sausages (add a pinch more cumin if sausages are not used). Remove and add to pot.

3. Pour a little water into the sautéing pan and scrape up all the lovely juices. Add to pot.

4. Now, to the ingredients in the soup pot add: 6 cups chicken stock (or half stock, half beer), 1-1½ cups dried split peas, several cloves garlic mashed, a pinch cayenne pepper. Simmer 1-2 hours until the peas are the consistency of a puree, then add 2-3 tbsp. nutritional yeast* and cook a few minutes longer. Salt and pepper to taste.

Accompany with a green salad, black bread and lager or ale.

SOUPE À L'OIGNON

Simple to prepare, yet a very rewarding soup.

6 <u>onions</u>, finely sliced

(optional: a slice or 2 of <u>streaky bacon</u>)

<u>Salt</u> and <u>pepper</u> to taste

5 cups <u>beef or vegetable stock</u>

a pinch of <u>sugar</u> and <u>paprika</u>

Sauté the onions (and bacon) in butter, oil or bacon fat slowly and gently until golden brown. When they are nearly cooked, sprinkle the sugar and paprika over them.

Add the stock. For a good onion soup it is essential to have a rich full-flavored stock.

Simmer 1½-2 hours. Taste for seasoning and add salt and pepper to taste.

To serve: Into each bowl place a slice of <u>gruyère or mozzarella</u>*<u>cheese</u> and a tbsp. or 2 of <u>dry sherry</u>. Now ladle in the steaming hot onion soup. Top with a slice of toasted (or oven-dried) <u>French bread</u> and a grating of <u>Parmesan cheese</u>.

Another serving suggestion from the old Parisian marketplace of Les Halles is to ladle the soup into a heat-proof tureen (or small individual ones), top with the toast, and gruyère and Parmesan cheeses, then bake in a 350° (mark 4) oven for 10 minutes, until the cheese is melty and bubbly.

Fortified with this soup, you can face winter with a smile.

OLD COUNTRY CABBAGE BORTSCH

Place in soup pot:
½ onion, chopped
½ cup chopped carrots
2 cups shredded
    raw beetroot
2 cups peeled
    tomatoes, cooked
    canned or raw
1 potato, cut-up

Cover with boiling
water and simmer
20 minutes.

Add: 1 tbsp. butter
    2 cups
    beef or
    vegetable
    stock
1 cup
shredded
cabbage
2 tbsp.
honey
1 tbsp.
vinegar
1 bay leaf

Simmer 15
or 20 minutes
longer.
    Add more
stock if a thinner
soup is desired, and
more beetroot for a
brighter colour.

Serve with
sour cream
and fresh
chopped dill.
Accompany
with black
bread,
spread
with sweet
(unsalted)
butter.

42

MINESTRONE AL PESTO

To a pot of boiling water add ¼–⅓ cup <u>white</u> <u>(Great Northern) beans</u>. Boil several minutes, remove from heat and let sit 1 hour. Return to heat and cook 1–1½ hours 'til tender. (If need be, substitute 1 medium-sized can of cooked red or kidney beans and eliminate the above process.)

Sauté 3 or 4 slices (chopped) of <u>salt pork or streaky</u> <u>bacon</u>. Add 1 chopped <u>onion</u> and cook 'til transparent.
Add and sauté a few minutes: 1 sliced <u>carrot</u>, 5 or 6 large ripe <u>tomatoes</u>, peeled and chopped, ¼–½ lb. cut <u>green beans</u> and (optional) <u>spinach</u>.

Then add 4-5 cups <u>beef or vegetable stock</u>, 1 <u>bay leaf</u>, 1 sprig fresh <u>rosemary</u> (2 or 3 inches) or a pinch dried rosemary. Let all come to the boil, then cover, turn down heat and simmer ½ hour or until all the vegetables are tender.

Add the already cooked (and drained) <u>beans</u>, a handful of <u>shell-shaped pasta</u>, 1 or 2 <u>zucchini</u> (courgettes), sliced, <u>salt</u> and freshly ground pepper to taste.

Simmer another 20 minutes or until the pasta and courgettes are tender. (This soup is excellent made a day before serving. If doing this, however, cook the pasta and courgettes in the soup immediately before serving.)

Serve this minestrone topped with a spoonful of <u>pesto sauce</u> and a sprinkling of freshly grated Parmesan cheese.

43

VIETNAMESE SOUP-SALAD

Soak ½ cup dried shrimp* in warm water about 10 minutes.

Sauté 1 lb. pork belly, cut into 2" x ½" x ⅛" slices, and 2 spring onions, chopped, for 5 minutes. Drain the shrimp and add to the pork-onion mixture; continue cooking 5 minutes more.

Add 1 tsp. salt and 3 large tomatoes, peeled and cut into sixths. Stir and cook 2 minutes more.

Add 2 cups of water and bring to the boil, then add 1 tbsp. fish sauce or gravy (NUOC mam*) and a dash of coarsely ground black pepper. Remove from the heat.

Makes 4 servings.

Soak ½ lb. rice noodles (look fun*) in warm water for 2 hours. Bring 6 cups water to the boil, add the noodles and boil for 5 minutes. Drain and set aside.

Wash and drain ¼ lb. mung bean sprouts (see seed sprouts or buy already sprouted), ½ cup fresh coriander leaves and ¼ cup fresh mint leaves. Slice or shred 6 or 7 lettuce leaves, and slice ½ peeled cucumber into ⅛ inch rounds, then cut into narrow strips. Set this aside also.

Chop coarsely ½ cup roasted peanuts and crush the contents of a small bag of corn chips* (optional). Place each in a little bowl.

Chop 2 spring onions, including the green part, and place in another small bowl. Heat 3 tbsp. oil and pour ~~n~~ over the onions. Let stand until cooled.

Now, to serve: place ¼ of the salad mixture in each bowl, then ¼ of the noodles, next a ladleful of the hot soup. Over this sprinkle the peanuts, corn chips and onion oil.

serve with chopsticks and spoons.

45

SALADS

PIÑATA SALAD

This multi-colored salad is named after the colorful candy-stuffed, paper-decorated animal shapes that are so much a part of the Mexican Christmas.

The piñata is hung from the ceiling and the children gather round. One of them is blind-folded, and he punches, swings and swats at the piñata, sometimes hitting his target.

Each child takes a turn and the one to smash it sends a cascade of candy tumbling to the feet of the scampering children.

48

Make a bed of shredded or finely
sliced lettuce.
Arrange on this:
    1 cup cold cooked roast beef or
        pork strips
    ½ - ¾ cup cold cooked red
        kidney beans
    1 sliced avocado
    1 or 2 sliced tomatoes
    1 sliced or chopped green pepper
      (sweet or hot, your choice)
    several slices orange (optional)
    Top with ½ cup grated cheddar cheese

Dress with this spicy dressing:
    2 parts light oil (soy, peanut, etc)
    1 part half vinegar, half lemon juice
    1 slice onion, minced
    1 tsp. each of cumin, oregano
      and paprika
    tiny pinch each sugar and cayenne
    salt and pepper to taste

Garnish with fresh coriander leaves and
serve with french bread or tortillas.*

SALADE NIÇOISE

Deriving its name from the town of Nice on the Côte d'Azur of France, our version of this salad consists of cold cooked and marinated vegetables on a bed of lettuce. The garnishes make this salad distinctive; the other ingredients can be changed at will and with the seasons.

1. In separate batches, steam cook approx. for 5 small, waxy potatoes, ½ lb. green beans, and several beetroots. When tender slice the potatoes and beetroots (¼ - ½ inch thick) and cut up the green beans.

2. Marinate each vegetable separately in a vinaigrette (approx. 2 parts oil to 1 of vinegar; we like olive oil). To the beetroot add a tsp. of honey. To the potatoes add a dash of a prepared mild mustard, some chopped parsley, basil and crushed garlic. Season the green beans with chopped parsley, savory, chives, and salt and pepper, each to taste, and let marinate several hours, overnight if possible.

3. Now arrange it all on a flat serving dish covered with a bed of lettucy greens.
Make individual mounds of each marinated vegetable and garnish with hard-cooked egg slices, Mediterranean-style black olives, tomato wedges, and fillets of anchovy and/or another salty fish such as tuna or smoked herring.

Sprinkle with chopped parsley and any other herb in season. Allow 1 whole egg and several olives, tomato wedges and anchovies per person. Fresh sweet green or red pepper is a good addition.

TABBOULÉH

An unusual salad from Lebanon, both refreshing and hearty. Perfect for a picnic! Serves 6.

1 cup bulgar wheat*
1 bunch spring onions, or 1 onion, minced

1½ cups parsley, chopped
2/3 cup fresh mint, chopped, or 2-3 tbsp. dried

1. Soak the bulgar wheat in water ½ hour. Drain well.

2. Mix the bulgar with the onions, pressing and squeezing with your hands to combine flavors.

3. Add parsley, mint, salt and pepper to taste, a dash allspice (optional). Dress with ¼ cup olive oil or to taste and the juice of 1-1½ lemons. Continue to toss and squeeze with your hands.

4. Line a serving platter with cooked vine leaves or raw cos lettuce leaves. Place a large mound of the bulgar wheat mixture on top and decorate with olives, tomatoes, cucumber slices, lemon wedges.

Yogurt is an excellent accompaniment.

51

GREEK SALAD

One of the most famous and typical dishes of Greece is the mixed salad.

Simply make a bed of raw salad greens, using lettuce when available, shredded cabbage when it's not. Add slices of cucumber, sweet green pepper rings, slices of raw onion. Garnish with several black Mediterranean-style olives, chunks of fetta cheese* and fresh tomato wedges. Dress with olive oil and lemon juice and dust with a good pinch oregano.

GARDEN SALAD

We like to accompany almost all meals with a fresh salad, either as a first course, California style, to get one's digestive juices flowing, or last, in the French way, to cleanse one's palate.

Whichever type of lettuce you choose, the most important thing is to wash each leaf and dry it well (a clean towel is good to use). There's nothing so distressing as a wet, limp salad, and careful drying will eliminate such a possibility.

The next thing to think of is temperature: not so cold as to be shocking, nor so warm as to be insipid, but perfectly chilled.

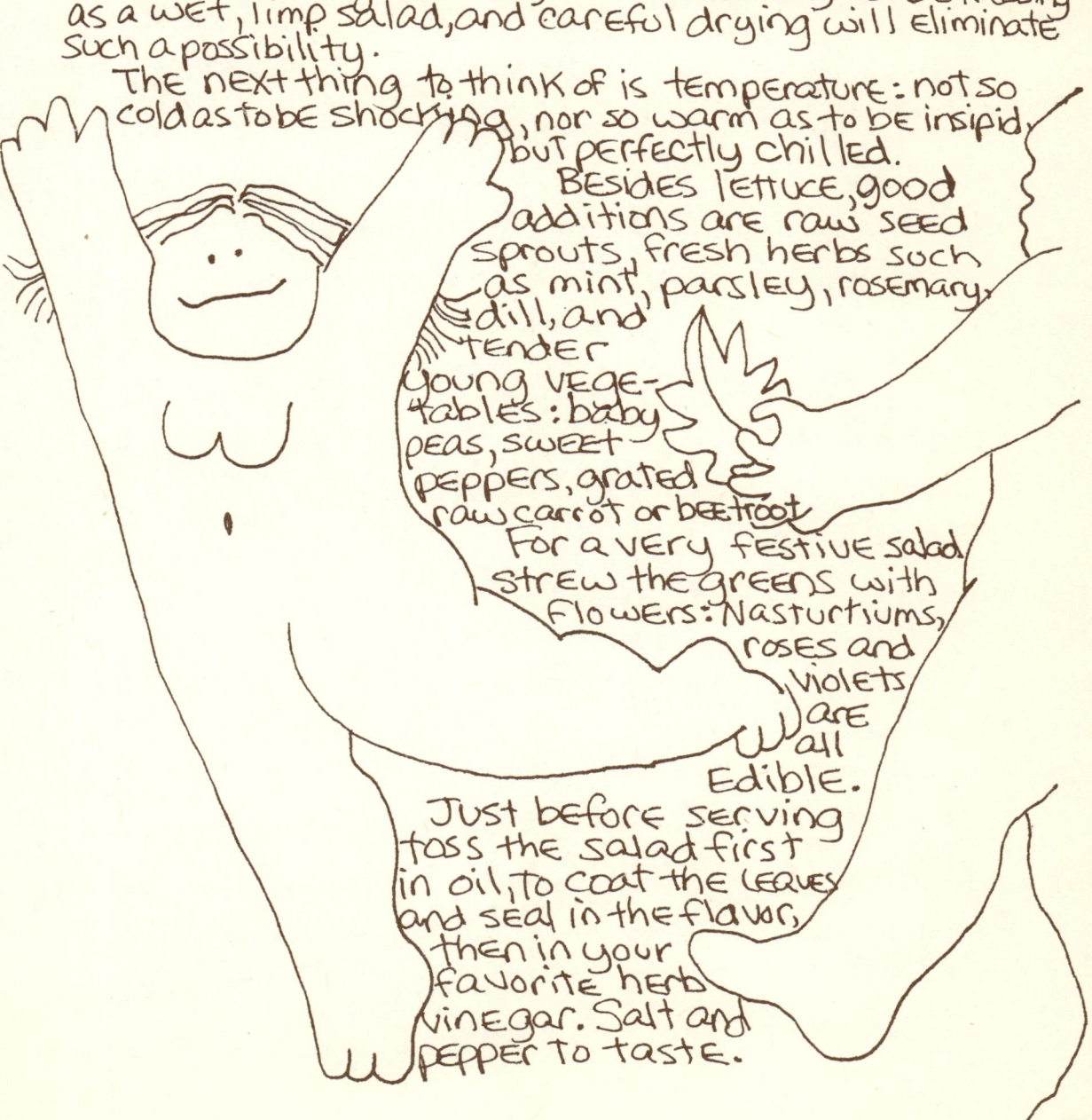

Besides lettuce, good additions are raw seed sprouts, fresh herbs such as mint, parsley, rosemary, dill, and tender young vege- tables: baby peas, sweet peppers, grated raw carrot or beetroot

For a very festive salad strew the greens with flowers: Nasturtiums, roses and violets are all edible.

Just before serving toss the salad first in oil, to coat the leaves and seal in the flavor, then in your favorite herb vinegar. Salt and pepper to taste.

ARABIC YOGURT SALAD

The measurements are all approximate and can be adjusted to suit your desires and ingredients.

Peel 1 cucumber. Slice into quarters lengthwise, then chop into ½ inch chunks. Sprinkle with salt and let sit ½ hour. This will extract the excess water and bitter juices.

Take a handful of chopped fresh mint or several tsp. dried mint. Combine this with the cucumber, 1 or 2 cloves of garlic, crushed, and about 1½-2 cups of yogurt.

A good salad to serve with cumin-roasted lamb (see our recipe Leg of Lamb, Desert Tribe Style).

ARABIC PARSLEY SALAD

Simply chop very finely 1 cup or so of parsley and combine it with the same amount of tahina sauce.

Serve garnished with olive oil and accompanied with french bread to spread the mixture on, as an hors d'oeuvre.

54

MARINATED CUCUMBERS

1. Slice 1 <u>onion</u> and several <u>cucumbers</u> very thinly. 2. Place in bowl and cover with a mild <u>vinegar</u> plus ½ cup or so <u>water</u>. 3. Add several tbsp. <u>raw sugar</u>*, a couple of pinches of <u>salt</u> and either a tsp. or so of prepared <u>mustard</u> or a good pinch <u>dill weed</u>. Let marinate for 1 or 2 hours.

A SALAD OF LETTUCE AND DILL

1. Choose a <u>green</u>, <u>leafy lettuce</u> (cos, or romaine). Rinse and dry.
2. Slice into thin (½ inch) strips.
3. Chop several <u>spring onions</u> and a nice bunch of <u>fresh dill</u>.

Toss together and dress with <u>olive oil</u> and <u>lemon juice</u> or <u>vinegar</u>. Sprinkle with a good pinch of <u>salt</u>.

# CUCUMBER SPEAR SALAD

This salad has a tangy fresh taste.

Take 1 unpeeled <u>cucumber</u> and cut it in half. Rub the cut ends together, against each other, in a friction-causing circular motion. The area that's being rubbed will foam a bit; this foam is the astringent liquid which many people find objectionable.

Cut off ¼ inch or so from each of the rubbed ends and discard them. Rinse off any remaining foam.

Peel the cucumbers and cut into spears. Dress with a dribble of <u>olive oil</u>, a squeeze of <u>lemon</u> and a sprinkling of <u>coarse salt</u>.

ANOTHER CUCUMBER AND YOGURT SALAD

Why not, since cucumber and yogurt go so well together?

Chop 1 peeled <u>cucumber</u> coarsely. Sprinkle with <u>salt</u> and leave 5-10 minutes, then rinse and dry.

Mix cucumber with 1 cup <u>yogurt</u>, ½ tsp. <u>tumeric</u>, and 1 or 2 mashed <u>garlic</u> cloves. Good with a spicy chicken curry or stuffed vine leaves.

AN ORANGE SALAD
From Morocco

Peel and slice 2 oranges and 1 red onion (or an ordinary one if not available). Arrange on a bed of lettuce and garnish with salty black olives and dress with olive oil and mixed herb vinegar. Enjoy with Moroccan Lamb and Eggplant.

FRENCH CELERY ROOT SALAD

An intriguing, unidentifiable flavor.

Grate 1 medium-sized celery root (celeriac or, in French, celeri-rave) using the large holes of the grater. Moisten with a little olive oil, dress with several tbsp. mayonnaise, flavored with 1 or 2 tsp. mild French mustard, and season with salt to taste.

Serve as a first course.

LEEKS VINAIGRETTE

Excellent with cold roast beef, poached fish or chicken, or as an addition to salade nicoise.

1. Into a pot of several cups boiling chicken stock, place a bunch or 2 of leeks (allow 1 medium-sized leek per person). Cover and simmer gently 'til tender (10-15 minutes, longer if large and tough) but not overdone.

2. Drain and save liquid for a soup.

3. Place leeks in a bowl and cover with a marinade of 1/4 cup olive oil, and 1/2 cup wine vinegar mixed with a tsp. prepared mild mustard and/or tarragon. Sprinkle with salt.

4. Let sit to marinate for several hours, rearranging the leeks every so often so that they all have a turn in the vinaigrette.

IMPORTANT: Leeks are grown in very sandy soil and should be rinsed very carefully. Slit each leek down the middle through the green leaves, then you can rinse the sand from between the leaves more easily. Cut off the root end and the tough greens; you're ready!

HORTA
(SPINACH OR WILD GREENS, GREEK STYLE)

Simply steam or boil several bunches of <u>spinach</u> until tender. Drain and let cool to room temperature.

Serve with a dressing of <u>olive oil</u> and <u>lemon juice</u> or <u>vinegar</u>.

Enjoy it with fresh crusty bread and a nice chunk of fetta cheese*.

Other greens such as <u>wild mustard</u>, <u>beet greens</u>, <u>nettle</u>, and <u>cabbage greens</u>, and Chinese greens such as <u>bok choy</u>, etc., may be treated this way, as may other vegetables such as <u>zucchini</u> (courgettes) <u>beetroot</u>, and <u>broad beans</u>.

IT is a very simple and refreshing dish, especially accompanying a more complicated meat and vegetable stew.

GRILLED PEPPERS

A simple dish favored throughout the Middle East, it is good as an hors d'oeuvre or as an accompaniment to brochettes (kebabs).

.Use 1 pepper for each 1 or 2 people. Choose a rich sweet red pepper if possible, otherwise a sweet yellow or green one.

Now grill the peppers over a flame until the skin chars and blackens (we use the flame on our gas stove). Place the peppers while hot either into a plastic bag (which you seal) or into a small pot (which you must lid tightly). Leave for 5-10 minutes—this steams it slightly and the skin should peel off easily, after being rinsed in cold water. Then halve the peppers and remove seeds and pith. Slice lengthwise into ½ inch wide slices.

Dress with olive oil, herbed vinegar or lemon juice and several crushed cloves of garlic. Salt and coarsely ground pepper to taste. Leave to sit at least 2 hours before serving.

Garnish with black Middle Eastern-style olives.

FRESH GREEN PEAS

The taste of fresh peas reminds us of a warm spring day.

To serve 4, allow about 2 lb. unshelled peas.

1. Shell peas. Blanch them by tossing into rapidly boiling water for 2-3 minutes, then removing from heat and draining immediately.

2. Melt 2 tbsp. (1oz.) butter in a saucepan and add 1 tbsp. minced onion. Sauté a minute, then add the peas, 1 head of cos lettuce, coarsely chopped, a dash each of salt and sugar, and several tbsp chicken stock or drippings. Cover and simmer on a low heat 5-10 minutes, depending on the size and age of the peas (this dish is best using the youngest, sweetest peas).

VARIATION:

Proceed as above for step 1, then place the blanched peas in a saucepan with several tbsp. each of stock (chicken, veal or beef) and tomato paste (or 3 or 4 fresh peeled tomatoes cooked down a bit). Add a dash each of sugar and salt, 1/4 tsp. oregano or sweet basil, 1 bay leaf, and 2-3 tbsp. fruity olive oil. Cover and simmer 15-20 minutes. This recipe is good for older, larger peas.

Do you grow your own peas? If you do, pick some of the tender early greens and eat raw, sprinkled with salt and vinegar, as an appetizer, as the peasants of Crete do.

JANE'S WINTER EGGPLANT
(AUBERGINE)

Sauté 2 sliced <u>onions</u> in olive oil a few minutes. Shake in a tsp. or more yellow <u>mustard seeds</u> and ½-1 tsp. <u>tumeric</u>. Put a lid on the pan if the seeds pop and splatter. Add 1 large or 2 small <u>eggplants</u> cut into approx. 1 inch cubes (before using eggplant, sprinkle the cubes with salt and let sit 15 minutes or so. Rinse, drain and proceed). Add 3 or 4 <u>tomatoes</u>, peeled if desired, and cut into wedges, and several tbsp. <u>stock</u>. Simmer uncovered until the eggplant is tender, adding more stock if the mixture becomes too dry. When it's finished cooking, add several tbsp. <u>tahina sauce</u> to the gravy. Serves 4.

Serve with additional tahina sauce and/or yogurt, and steamed brown rice or crusty bread. Accompanied with a fresh green salad this makes a satisfying vegetarian meal.

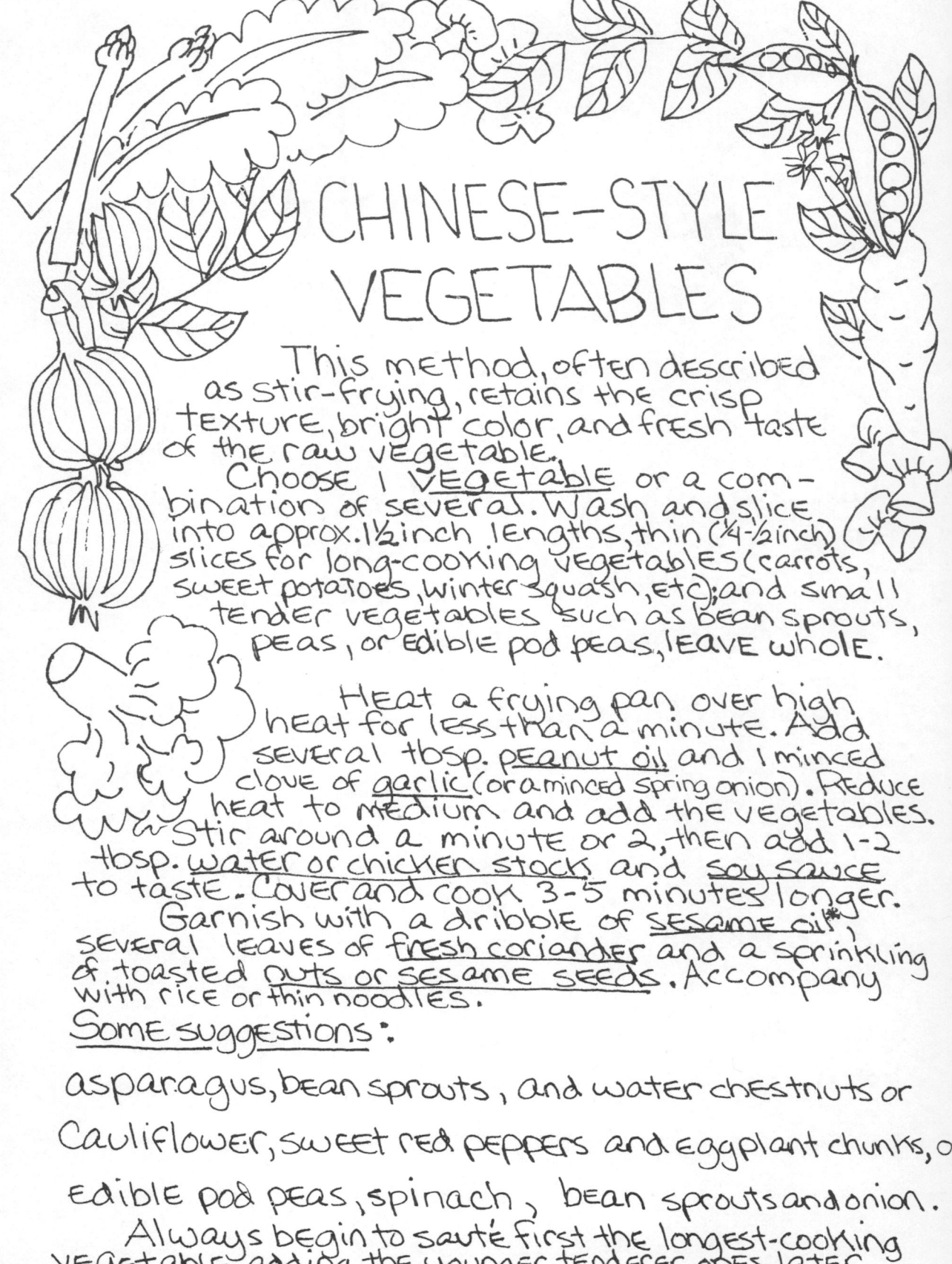

CHINESE-STYLE VEGETABLES

This method, often described as stir-frying, retains the crisp texture, bright color, and fresh taste of the raw vegetable.

Choose 1 VEGETABLE or a combination of several. Wash and slice into approx. 1½ inch lengths, thin (¼-½ inch) slices for long-cooking vegetables (carrots, sweet potatoes, winter squash, etc); and small tender vegetables such as bean sprouts, peas, or edible pod peas, leave whole.

Heat a frying pan over high heat for less than a minute. Add several tbsp. peanut oil and 1 minced clove of garlic (or a minced spring onion). Reduce heat to medium and add the vegetables. Stir around a minute or 2, then add 1-2 tbsp. water or chicken stock and soy sauce to taste. Cover and cook 3-5 minutes longer.

Garnish with a dribble of sesame oil, several leaves of fresh coriander and a sprinkling of toasted nuts or sesame seeds. Accompany with rice or thin noodles.

Some suggestions:

asparagus, bean sprouts, and water chestnuts or

Cauliflower, sweet red peppers and eggplant chunks, or

edible pod peas, spinach, bean sprouts and onion.

Always begin to sauté first the longest-cooking vegetable, adding the younger, tenderer ones later.

BUTTER-BROWNED POTATOES

Choose the smallest <u>new potatoes</u> you can find. Wash, then boil or steam until barely tender but still firm.

Remove the potatoes from the heat; drain and peel them.

In a frying pan melt several tbsp. sweet (unsalted) <u>butter</u> until hot but not brown. Place the potatoes in the pan, keeping them whole and turning as each side becomes golden brown.

Garnish with minced parsley and/or a sprinkle of paprika.

Once we prepared a dinner in the home of some Greek friends in Crete. They were highly skeptical about bortsch and outright suspicious of the potato pancakes.

Both of us had several people gathered tightly around us, muttering in Greek and looking quizzically at each other, as we busied ourselves preparing the food.

When the meal was finally served the diners approached the table with great trepidation; maybe they would have a "little taste" in the name of friendship.

As the "little tastes" were attended to, appetites blossomed. Soon the huge mound of crisp brown potato discs had disappeared, leaving but a trace of crumbs; the bowls, tell-tale red from the bortsch, were empty. The meal had been a success!

Wine was poured out, glasses clicked, and our friends made this toast: "We will translate your cookbook into Greek!"

POTATO PANCAKES
(LATKES)

6 large or 10 medium-sized <u>potatoes</u>   1 <u>onion</u>

2 beaten <u>eggs</u>   <u>flour</u>

<u>salt</u>, <u>pepper</u>, a pinch of <u>sugar</u>

    Grate the potato and onion in the small holes of the grater. Stir in the eggs, salt, pepper, sugar. Thicken with flour to the consistency of a thick batter (not too runny).

    Drop by tbsp. into a frying pan containing 1/4 inch <u>hot oil</u>. Turn when edges are brown and crispy. Drain on a paper and serve with <u>sour cream</u>, <u>yogurt</u> or <u>apple sauce</u>.

ZUCCHINI PANCAKES

1 lb. <u>zucchini</u> (courgettes)   1/2 onion

2 <u>potatoes</u>   <u>flour</u>

<u>salt</u>, <u>pepper</u>, dash of sugar   2 beaten <u>eggs</u>

1/2-1 tsp. <u>sweet basil</u>   1 clove <u>garlic</u>

    Grate the zucchini, onion and potato on the large holes of the grater. Sprinkle with salt and set in a colander to drain the excess liquid; leave for 5 minutes or so.

    Take half of the vegetable mixture and purée it (an electric blender works very well). Recombine the 2 mixtures, add the egg and flour to make a thick batter. Fry as for potato pancakes.

CHEESE FONDUE

This dish originated in Switzerland many years ago. Both cheese and bread were made in the summer and fall to last through the winter. The bread became very hard and the cheese had to be warmed over a fire to soften. Someone discovered that wine melted with the cheese was tasty. During the winter months the peasants would gather round the fire and each would dip his share of bread into the cheese mixture.

1 Lb. combination emmenthal and gruyère
2 cups dry white wine
3 level tbsp. flour
Fresh grated nutmeg
1 clove garlic, minced
1 large loaf stale french bread
3 tbsp. Kirsch

1. Grate cheese, toss with flour (occasionally we add such herbs as basil or tarragon at this point).
2. Cube bread (approx. 1½ inches), then toast in oven.
3. Heat wine over stove. When hot but not boiling, slowly add cheese mixture, stirring constantly with a wooden spoon until cheese is melted. (A favorite variation in Swiss homes is to add 2 peeled and coarsely chopped tomatoes when the cheese has melted.) Now add the Kirsch.

Serve and keep warm over a fondue burner (spirit lamp). Each person spears a bread cube, dunks and swirls it in the fondue, then pops it into his mouth. Accompany with a tossed green salad and chilled apple juice. Serves 4.

According to Swiss custom, the first person to lose his chunk of bread in the cheese mixture must kiss each person at the table.

70

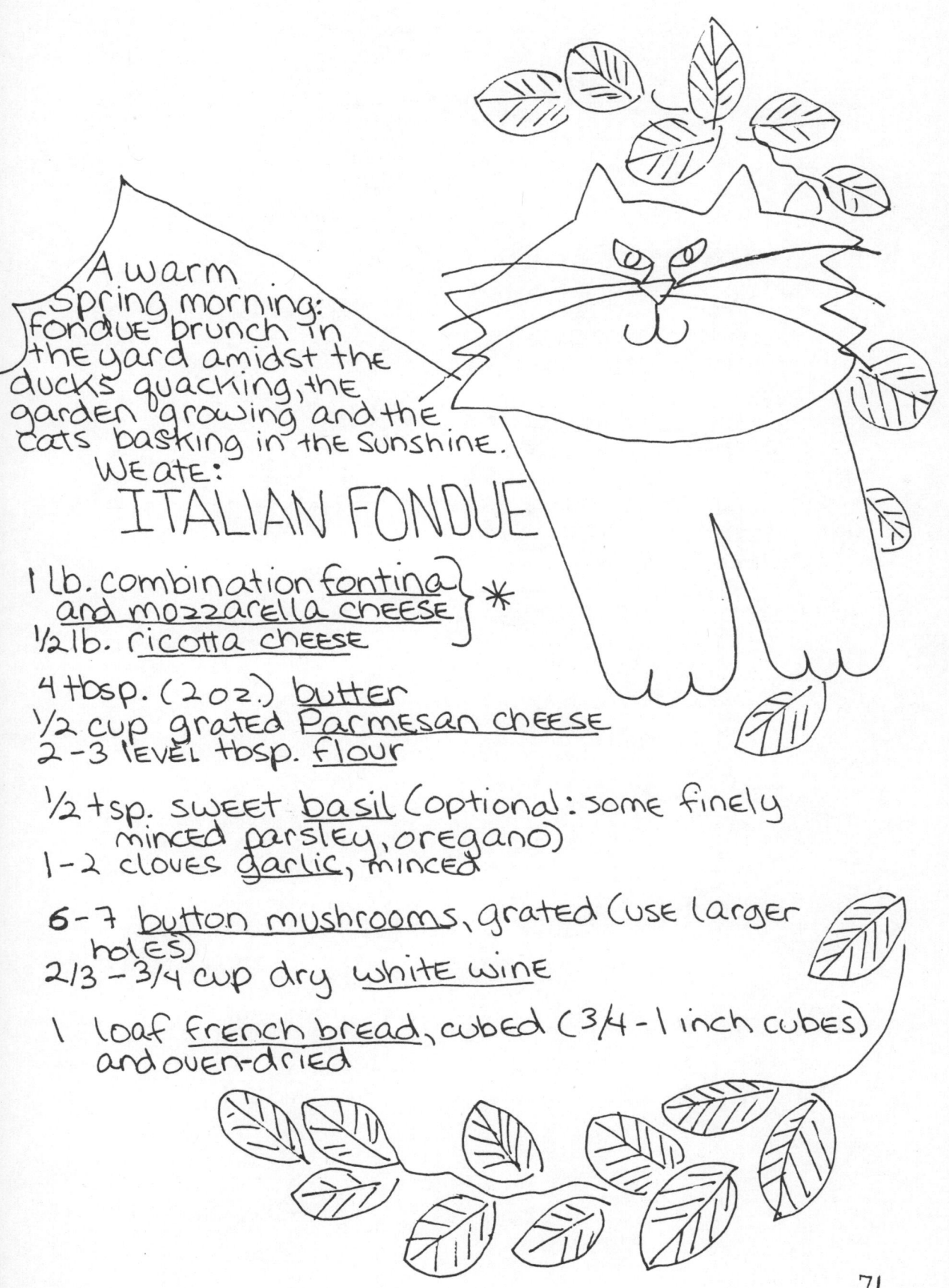

A warm spring morning: fondue brunch in the yard amidst the ducks quacking, the garden growing and the cats basking in the sunshine. We ate:

ITALIAN FONDUE

1 lb. combination <u>fontina</u> and <u>mozzarella cheese</u> } *
½ lb. <u>ricotta cheese</u>

4 tbsp. (2 oz.) <u>butter</u>
½ cup grated <u>Parmesan cheese</u>
2-3 level tbsp. <u>flour</u>

½ tsp. sweet <u>basil</u> (optional: some finely minced parsley, oregano)
1-2 cloves <u>garlic</u>, minced

6-7 <u>button mushrooms</u>, grated (use larger holes)
2/3 - 3/4 cup dry <u>white wine</u>

1 loaf <u>french bread</u>, cubed (3/4 - 1 inch cubes) and oven-dried

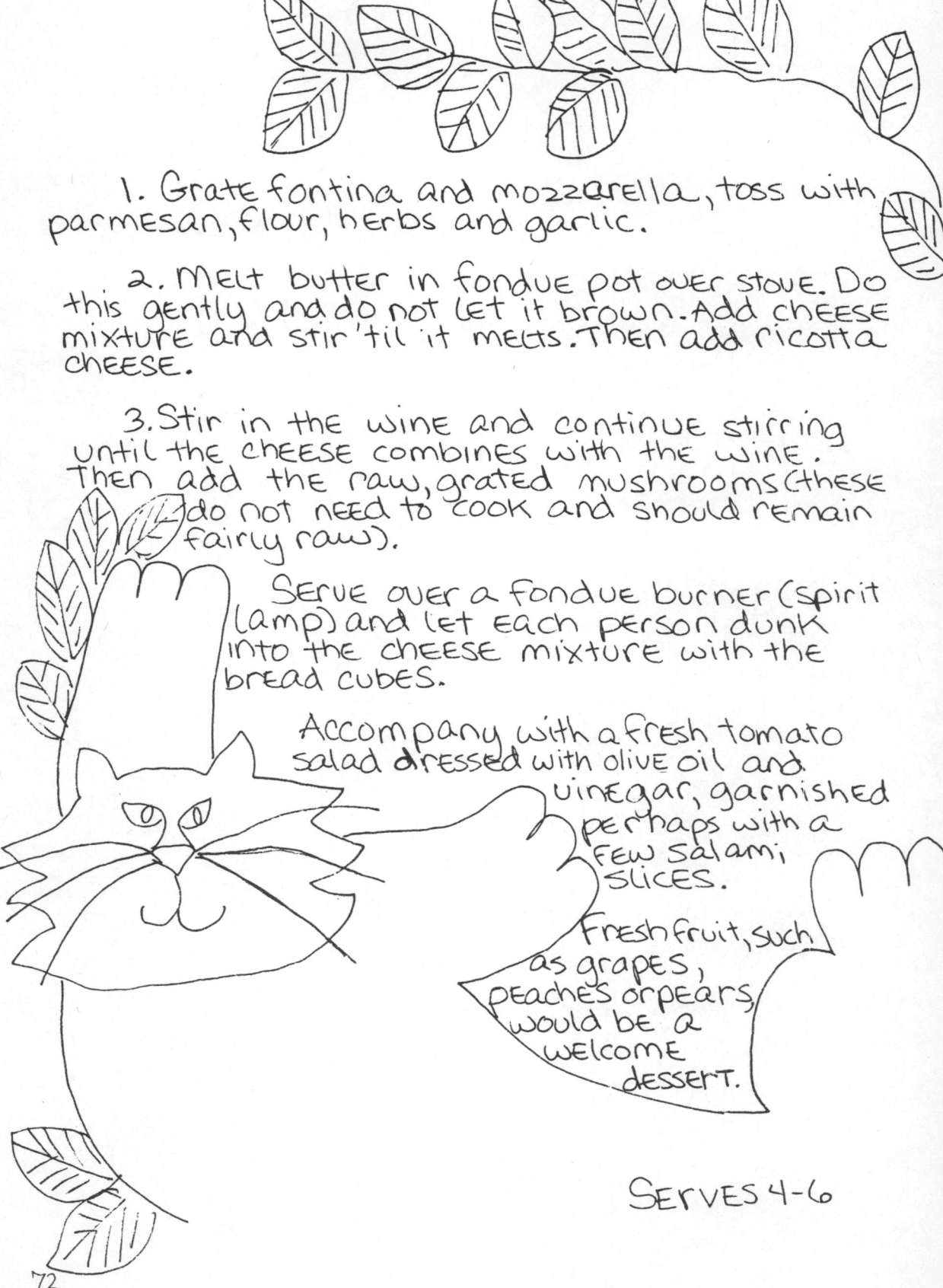

1. Grate fontina and mozzarella, toss with parmesan, flour, herbs and garlic.

2. Melt butter in fondue pot over stove. Do this gently and do not let it brown. Add cheese mixture and stir 'til it melts. Then add ricotta cheese.

3. Stir in the wine and continue stirring until the cheese combines with the wine. Then add the raw, grated mushrooms (these do not need to cook and should remain fairly raw).

Serve over a fondue burner (spirit lamp) and let each person dunk into the cheese mixture with the bread cubes.

Accompany with a fresh tomato salad dressed with olive oil and vinegar, garnished perhaps with a few salami slices.

Fresh fruit, such as grapes, peaches or pears, would be a welcome dessert.

SERVES 4-6

FETTA CHEESE OMELETTE

This dish is a favorite of peasants in Crete. The recipe serves 4.

1. Take ⅓-½ lb. fetta cheese* and cut into 1 inch cubes.

2. Beat 8 eggs lightly with ½ tsp. water.

3. Heat several tbsp. olive oil in a frying pan. When hot and barely smoking, add the beaten eggs. Cook over a moderately high heat, gently pulling up the cooked edges and tipping the pan to allow the liquid egg to run under. When barely set, add the cheese chunks.

4. When bottom is golden brown, take off stove and place under broiler (grill). Leave 'til the top turns golden brown, just a minute or so; or flip instead and fry other side.

Serve with crusty bread and salty black Greek style olives.

CHILLIES RELLEÑOS
Mexican stuffed peppers

Choose either the large green chilli peppers, mild and not too fiery, or the more available sweet green peppers.

<u>To prepare peppers</u>: Allow 1 or 2 per person; place them under the broiler (grill) and grill on both sides until blistered. Put peppers into a plastic bag or a small pot with a tight-fitting lid. Seal and leave about 10 minutes. The steam will penetrate the peppers and the skin will peel off easily. When peeled, discard the seeds and pith and the peppers are ready for stuffing.

<u>To stuff</u>: The simplest and our favorite way is to use cheese (wensleydale, cheddar or gruyère would be fine). It melts beautifully and mellowly. Simply cut an appropriate-sized piece of cheese and place it inside the pepper.

Another filling is picadillo, a minced meat preparation. Fill each pepper with several tbsp. of the mixture.

<u>The batter</u>: Separate several <u>eggs</u> (allow 1 egg per 2 or 3 chillies). Beat the whites until not quite stiff; lightly beat the yolks and add a spoon or so <u>flour</u> to make a light paste. Combine both mixtures, <u>salt</u> to taste.

<u>To cook</u>: Dip each stuffed pepper first in <u>flour</u> (and shake off the excess), then into the batter, then into 1½-2 inches <u>hot oil</u>. Fry until golden brown on one side, then turn and fry the other side.

<u>Serving</u>: Serve with tomato sauce, a dollop of sour cream, a garnish of coriander leaves, and frijoles refritos.

<u>Picadillo</u>: Sauté 1 chopped <u>onion</u> and 1 clove <u>garlic</u> until limp. Add ½-⅔ lb. <u>minced beef</u>, and stir as it fries. Season with <u>cinnamon</u>, <u>cloves</u>, and a dash each of <u>cumin</u>, <u>cayenne pepper</u> and <u>salt</u>. Add ¼ cup each <u>raisins</u> and coarsely chopped <u>nuts</u> (peanuts, almonds or cashews), 2 tbsp. <u>tomato paste</u>, ⅓ cup <u>dry sherry</u> or <u>dry red wine</u>, 1 or 2 tbsp. <u>honey</u>, and several sprigs fresh <u>coriander leaves</u>, chopped (optional). Simmer 10-15 minutes. Good also wrapped in a tortilla* as a taco (see Frijoles Refritos).

75

SPANAKOPITA

This Greek spinach and cheese pie makes an excellent luncheon dish.

Sauté ½-1 onion, chopped, in olive oil until transparent. Add 2 lb. fresh, washed and chopped spinach and cook, covered for 10 minutes. Uncover and cook over a high heat a few minutes until most of the liquid has evaporated and the spinach begins to stick.

Remove from heat and add 2 tsp. dried dillweed (or 1½ tbsp. fresh dill), a grating of nutmeg, salt and pepper to taste, 1 cup (½ lb.) cottage or ricotta* cheese, ⅓ lb. crumbled Fetta cheese*, 1 or 2 spring onions (including the tender green part), and 1 large or 2 small eggs, beaten.

Brush the bottom and sides of a 9"x9"x2" baking dish with melted butter. Place 1 layer of filo dough (see filo dough pastries) in it with the edges overlapping the sides. Brush with melted butter; repeat until you have 4 or 5 layers. Now add the spinach-cheese mixture. Top with 4 or 5 more layers filo dough, tucking the loose ends between layers, brushing each sheet with melted butter.

Bake in a 325°-350°(mark 3-4) oven for 35-40 minutes until crisp and brown.

SERVES 6.

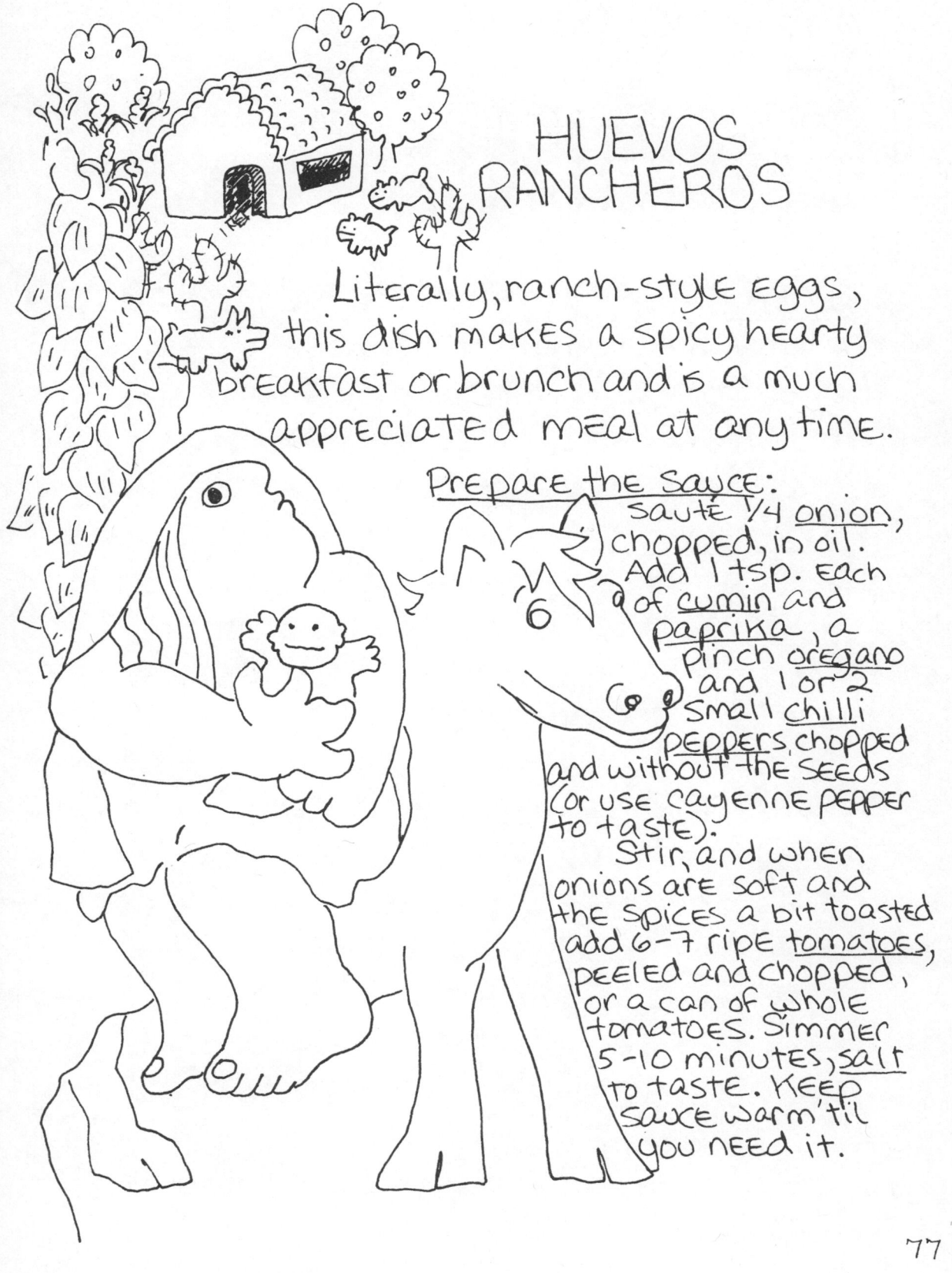

HUEVOS RANCHEROS

Literally, ranch-style eggs, this dish makes a spicy hearty breakfast or brunch and is a much appreciated meal at any time.

Prepare the sauce:
Sauté 1/4 onion, chopped, in oil. Add 1 tsp. Each of cumin and paprika, a pinch oregano and 1 or 2 small chilli peppers, chopped and without the seeds (or use cayenne pepper to taste).
Stir, and when onions are soft and the spices a bit toasted add 6-7 ripe tomatoes, peeled and chopped, or a can of whole tomatoes. Simmer 5-10 minutes, salt to taste. Keep sauce warm 'til you need it.

77

Cook the eggs: poach 8 eggs (allow 2 per person) according to taste. The yolks should be quite runny.

Warm the tortillas*: place several at a time in a frying pan with a dab of fat. Cover to retain moisture and heat gently. They may also be sautéed. Allow 1 per person.

Assemble: place 1 warm tortilla on each plate and 2 eggs on top. Spoon several tbsp. of the sauce over the eggs and top with several sprigs of fresh coriander. Serves 4.

Garnishes and accompaniments to this dish may include chorizos* (spicy sausages), pickled chilli peppers, avocado slices, frijoles refritos (refried beans), green salad.

Drink a strong, chilled lager alongside.

SAN FRANCISCO FIREHOUSE SPECIAL

NO ONE is sure exactly how this dish originated, though all agree it was concocted in San Francisco during the early years of this century. Some say it was first prepared by the Italian immigrants as a variation on the frittata or Italian omelette, while others maintain that it was born in a firehouse and quickly became regular fare of the firemen, its fame soon spreading to the rest of the community.

For 4 persons allow 1 lb. minced beef, 1 cup cooked, drained and coarsely chopped spinach, ½ onion, chopped, and (optional) ¼ lb. or less mushrooms, halved.

Sauté the onions in butter or olive oil 'til limp, add the meat and cook, stirring until it loses its pinkness. Add the spinach, mushrooms and a large pinch sweet basil, a grating of nutmeg and 1 crushed clove of garlic. Salt and pepper to taste.

Turn up the heat a little and add 4 eggs beaten with 1 tsp. cream or water. Stir occasionally and cook until eggs are set but not overcooked!

Serve with French bread and a leafy green salad.

EGGS BENEDICT

This rich and satisfying dish is a favorite of many West Coast Americans for late breakfasts on Sundays or special occasions.

Allow per person ½ split <u>muffin</u>, toasted and buttered. Top with a slice of lean pan-browned (fried) <u>bacon</u> then on top of that 1 poached <u>egg</u> (hint: add a dash salt and vinegar to the poaching water for firmer, less ragged eggs).

Crown with 2 or 3 tbsp. <u>hollandaise sauce</u> and accompany with poached <u>asparagus</u> or <u>broccoli</u>, and perhaps the day is special enough for champagne and strawberries.

BRIK À L'OEUF

Golden, flaky gossamer-thin layers, with a gush of delicate egg yolk bursting through on the first bite.

This pastry is from Tunisia. It is quick and simple to make and positively delicious.

For each brik use 1 sheet of <u>filo dough</u>, folded in half.

Place in 1 corner of the rectangle a tsp. of <u>tuna fish</u> or several anchovy pieces, and ½–1 tsp. each of <u>chopped parsley</u> and <u>raw chopped onion</u>, then break a <u>raw egg</u> onto it.

Quickly and carefully fold in a triangular shape (it's a good idea to practise the technique of forming these pastries first with a piece of paper — see filo dough pastries) and fry in approx. 4 inches hot oil. The outside should be golden brown and crisp, but be careful not to break or overcook the egg.

Serve accompanied by the following sauce:
<u>Harissa</u>
Place ½ cup water, 2 tbsp. paprika, 2 tsp. cumin, 1 tsp. cayenne pepper and a pinch salt in a saucepan and heat until very hot but not boiling. Stir, remove from heat. Taste for seasoning — it should be very spicy and potent. If desired, fresh chopped coriander leaves may be added before serving.

PASTA and RICE KA GRAINS

PASTA

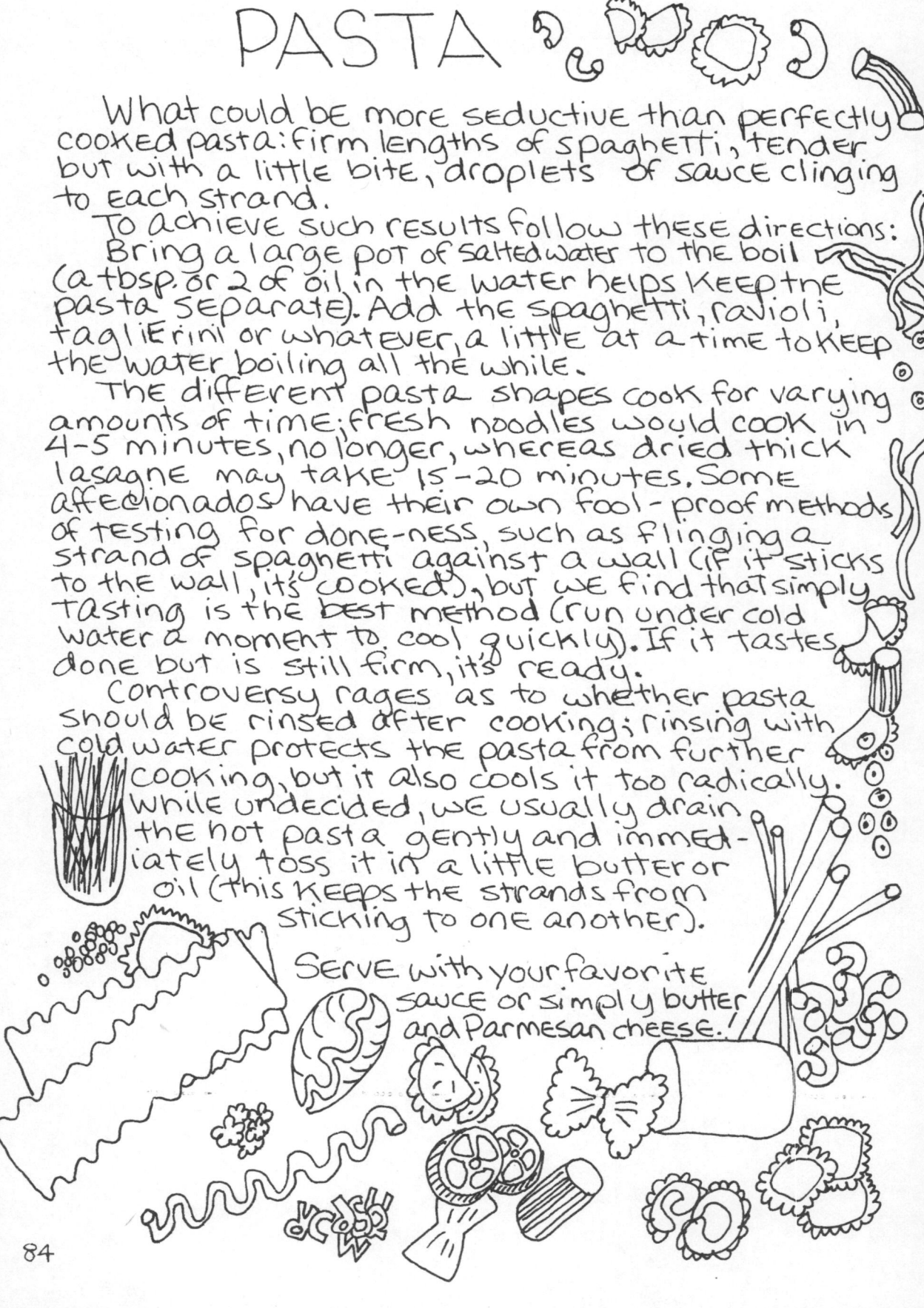

What could be more seductive than perfectly cooked pasta: firm lengths of spaghetti, tender but with a little bite, droplets of sauce clinging to each strand.

To achieve such results follow these directions:

Bring a large pot of salted water to the boil (a tbsp. or 2 of oil in the water helps keep the pasta separate). Add the spaghetti, ravioli, taglierini or whatever, a little at a time to keep the water boiling all the while.

The different pasta shapes cook for varying amounts of time: fresh noodles would cook in 4-5 minutes, no longer, whereas dried thick lasagne may take 15-20 minutes. Some affecionados have their own fool-proof methods of testing for done-ness, such as flinging a strand of spaghetti against a wall (if it sticks to the wall, it's cooked), but we find that simply tasting is the best method (run under cold water a moment to cool quickly). If it tastes done but is still firm, it's ready.

Controversy rages as to whether pasta should be rinsed after cooking; rinsing with cold water protects the pasta from further cooking, but it also cools it too radically. While undecided, we usually drain the hot pasta gently and immediately toss it in a little butter or oil (this keeps the strands from sticking to one another).

Serve with your favorite sauce or simply butter and Parmesan cheese!

84

SPAGHETTI SAUCE

When David was a little boy he had a grown-up friend, Tony the Shoeshine man, who bought little David a shoeshining kit to follow in his footsteps.

David shined 3 pairs of shoes, then retired, but he still makes a tasty spaghetti sauce, learned, he says, at Tony's knee.

① Chop 1 <u>onion</u> and ½ <u>sweet green pepper</u>. Sauté in olive oil or streaky bacon fat 'til golden. Add 1 lb. <u>minced beef</u> or ½ beef, ½ sausage meat. Stir and continue sautéing.

② Put mixture in a large pot and add: 12 large ripe peeled <u>tomatoes</u> or a 16-oz. can of cooked tomatoes.

③ Add: several tins <u>tomato paste</u>, several cups liquid (stock or red wine).

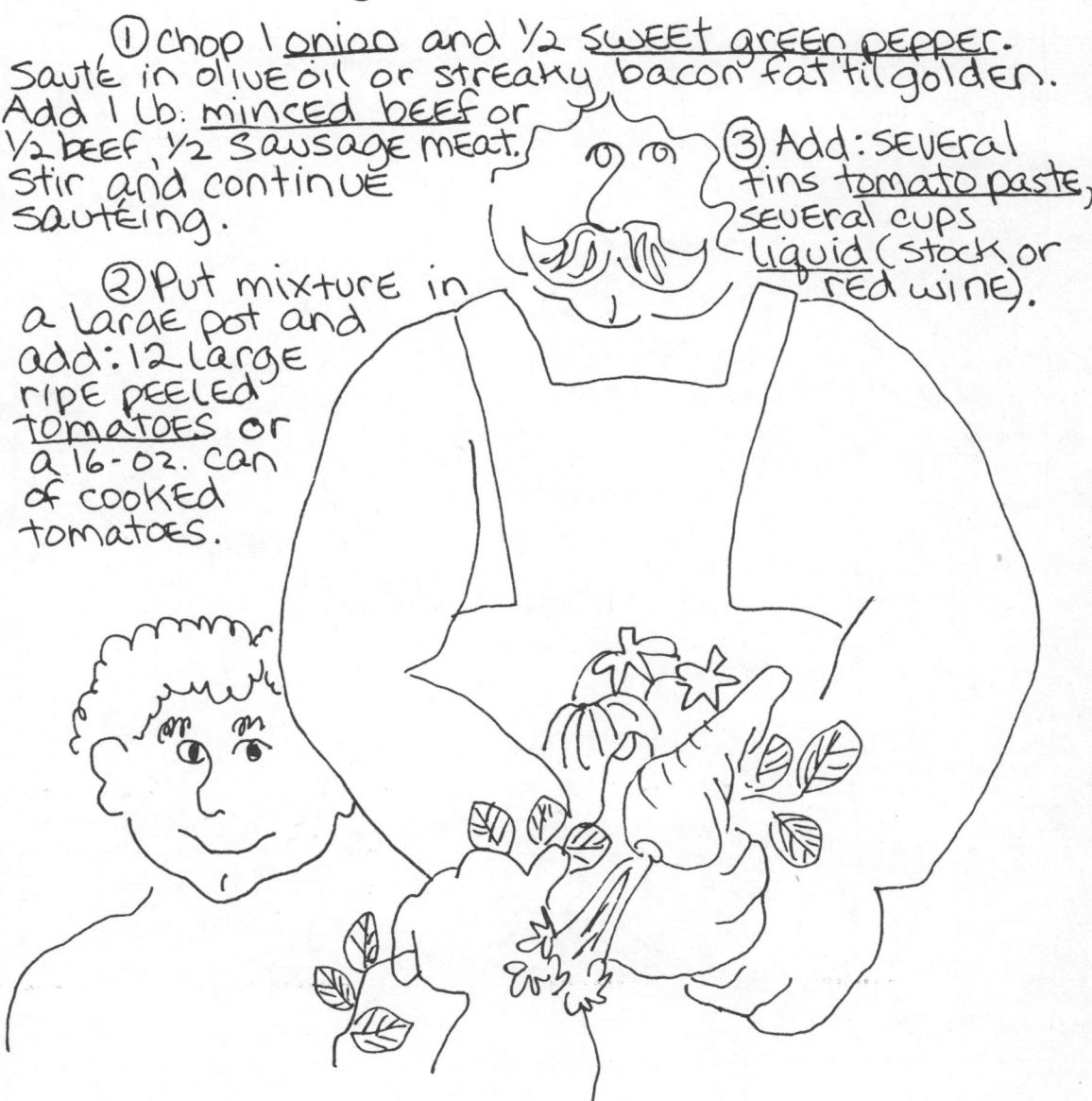

85

④ Also add ½ cup <u>olive oil</u>, 1 cup chopped <u>button mushrooms</u>, lots of fresh <u>parsley</u>, chopped, several cloves of <u>garlic</u>, and approx. 1 cup of a <u>vegetable combination</u>: a little chopped carrot, some spinach, celery, green beans, or any other vegetable you wish!

Season the sauce with <u>marjoram</u>, <u>oregano</u>, <u>basil</u>, <u>thyme</u>, <u>fennel seed</u>, <u>salt</u> and <u>black pepper</u>. Add a dash of <u>worcester sauce</u> and <u>catsup</u> (ketchup) or substitute 2 tsp. honey or sugar.

The most important ingredient is a long slow simmer, 6 hours at least; all day is better. Add stock or wine as needed, if the sauce becomes too thick.

Serve over thin spaghetti freshly cooked until barely tender, or "al dente". Pass a bowl of freshly grated Parmesan cheese and accompany with an antipasto of olives, marinated beans or artichokes, raw carrot sticks and a crisp green salad, following with a small selection of cheeses (a Bel Paese and Fontina would be nice). To drink, choose a vigorous wine such as Chianti.

Serves 10 or so.

EGGPLANT (AUBERGINE) SPAGHETTI I

1. Cut into cubes 1 large <u>eggplant</u>, salt and leave for ½ hour. Then rinse, drain, and dry.

2. Sauté in olive oil until golden 1 chopped <u>onion</u>. Add several cloves <u>garlic</u>, 1 <u>bay leaf</u>, and 2 or 3 lb. <u>tomatoes</u>, peeled and chopped. Then add 1 small tin <u>tomato paste</u>, the cubed <u>eggplant</u>, a pinch each of <u>oregano</u> and <u>sugar</u>, and a handful of Mediterranean-style <u>black olives</u>, stoned.

3. Add several cups of <u>water</u>, <u>chicken stock</u> or <u>red wine</u> (or combination), a handful of chopped <u>parsley</u>, <u>salt</u> and <u>pepper</u> to taste. Simmer un-covered 1 hour or so.

Serve on thin spaghetti with a sprinkling of grated Parmesan cheese. Serves 4-6.

EGGPLANT (AUBERGINE) SPAGHETTI II

SERVES 4-6.

<u>MAKE A SAUCE</u>: sauté in olive oil, butter, or streaky bacon fat 'til golden 1 chopped <u>onion</u>. Add 4 or 5 cloves <u>garlic</u> and 10-15 <u>tomatoes</u> (PEELED IF DESIRED; USE CANNED IF OUT OF SEASON). Stir and add 1 small can <u>tomato paste</u>, SEVERAL cups of <u>chicken stock</u> (or ½ water and ½ red wine) and a bit of chopped <u>bacon</u> (optional). Simmer an hour or so. <u>Salt</u> and <u>pepper</u> to taste.

~ ❀ ~

<u>MEANWHILE</u>: SLICE 1 large or several small <u>eggplants</u> in ¼ inch thick slices. PLACE in a colander, sprinkle with salt and LEAVE for ½ hour. Rinse, drain and dry the eggplant and sauté the slices in olive oil a few minutes until tender. KEEP warm in a low oven 'til serving.

Cook 1 - 1½ lb. thin spaghetti.

~ ❀ ~

<u>PRESENTATION</u>: arrange eggplant around the edge of the platter. In the CENTER make a mound of spaghetti. Top with the tomato sauce and a handful of chopped parsley and basil. Offer a bowl of grated Parmesan cheese alongside, and if desired SERVE with small meatballs.

88

CRAB SPAGHETTI

Cook 1 lb. Japanese style buckwheat noodles* or thin wholewheat spaghetti in salted boiling water until "al dente" or just barely tender. Drain, then toss with butter.

Meanwhile melt 2 tbsp. (1 oz.) of sweet (unsalted) butter and gently sauté 1/4-1/3 lb. of crabmeat. Add 1/2-3/4 cup cooked green peas, and the cooked spaghetti.

Toss the mixture with butter and 1/2 cup or so grated Parmesan cheese. Salt and pepper to taste.

Drink white wine or chilled apple juice and accompany with cucumber spear salad. Serves 4.

BROWN RICE

Brown rice is the whole grain of the rice. The brown color is the edible covering and is rich in nutrition, especially the B vitamins.

Prepare thusly: rinse 1 cup brown rice to rid it of any grit or talc (a fine powder often added to packaged rice).

Place the rice and 2 cups water into a pot; add a pinch of salt and/or soy sauce.

Cover pot with lid and place on a fairly high heat until the water boils, then turn down heat and simmer gently 'til tender, approx. 40 minutes. Do not remove lid during the cooking as it allows steam to escape and interferes with the steaming process.

Serve with butter or soy sauce.

Leftover rice is especially good in stuffed vine leaves or fried with vegetables, Chinese style.

PAELLA

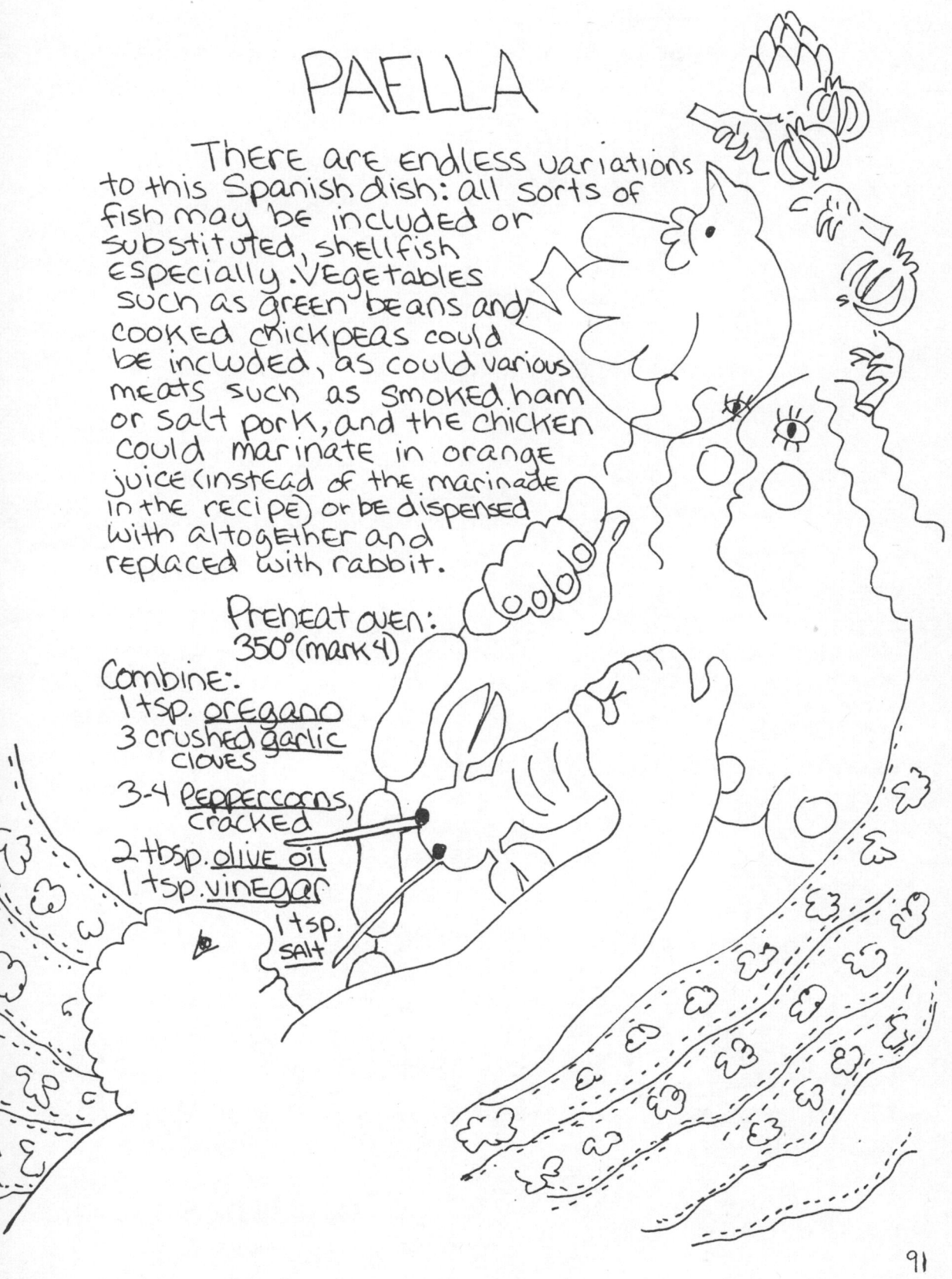

There are endless variations to this Spanish dish: all sorts of fish may be included or substituted, shellfish especially. Vegetables such as green beans and cooked chickpeas could be included, as could various meats such as smoked ham or salt pork, and the chicken could marinate in orange juice (instead of the marinade in the recipe) or be dispensed with altogether and replaced with rabbit.

Preheat oven:
350° (mark 4)

Combine:
1 tsp. oregano
3 crushed garlic cloves
3-4 peppercorns, cracked
2 tbsp. olive oil
1 tsp. vinegar
1 tsp. salt

Pour mixture over 1 jointed <u>chicken</u>. Toss and let sit 1 hour, then brown in olive oil.

Add to pan and sauté 5 minutes:

chopped { 1 <u>chorizo</u>*(spanish sausage)
1 <u>onion</u>

sliced { 1 <u>sweet red pepper</u>
1 <u>sweet green pepper</u>

1 tsp. ground <u>coriander seed</u>

After sautéing, add ⅓ cup <u>tomato sauce</u> (or several ripe, peeled tomatoes and 1 tsp. tomato paste) and 1-1½ cups <u>brown rice</u> which has been precooked 20-25 minutes, then drained.

Mix it all together over the heat, cooking a few minutes. Then add 1½ - 2 cups <u>chicken stock</u>, 1 large pinch <u>saffron</u>, and approx. 1 lb. shelled and cleaned <u>shellfish</u> such as shrimps, scallops, crab, mussels (some may be included with their shells, in this case allow more weight). Small fresh sardines would be good included now, as would any fish chunks, trimmed of bones and skin.

Continuing over the heat, add 1 cup fresh (precooked) canned or frozen <u>green peas</u>, and 1 jar of marinated <u>artichoke hearts</u> (or several green olives sliced and 2 tsp. capers).

Bake covered about 25 minutes or until the rice is tender and the chicken done. Place 8-10 <u>clams</u> (or mussels or oysters) on top of the rice mixture and return covered to the oven. Leave about 10 minutes or until the clams pop open.

Accompany with a tossed green salad and a dry white wine. Serves 6.

PILAFF

Serves 4-5.

Sauté or toast ½ cup almonds in a little butter until browned. Set aside.

Sauté a handful of un-cooked, broken up vermicelli* pieces. When golden, remove from pan and set aside. Sauté 1 cup raw brown rice in a little butter until the kernels are golden.

Combine rice, nuts, ⅓-½ cup raisins, vermicelli pieces and 2 cups chicken stock or salted water. Cover, bring to the boil, then reduce heat and simmer 30-40 minutes, until rice is tender.

Meanwhile sauté 2 sliced onions and 1-2 garlic cloves in butter with a pinch of cinnamon until very limp.

Fork onion mixture into cooked rice and serve with yogurt, roasted lamb in a spicy sauce or tiny fried fish.

93

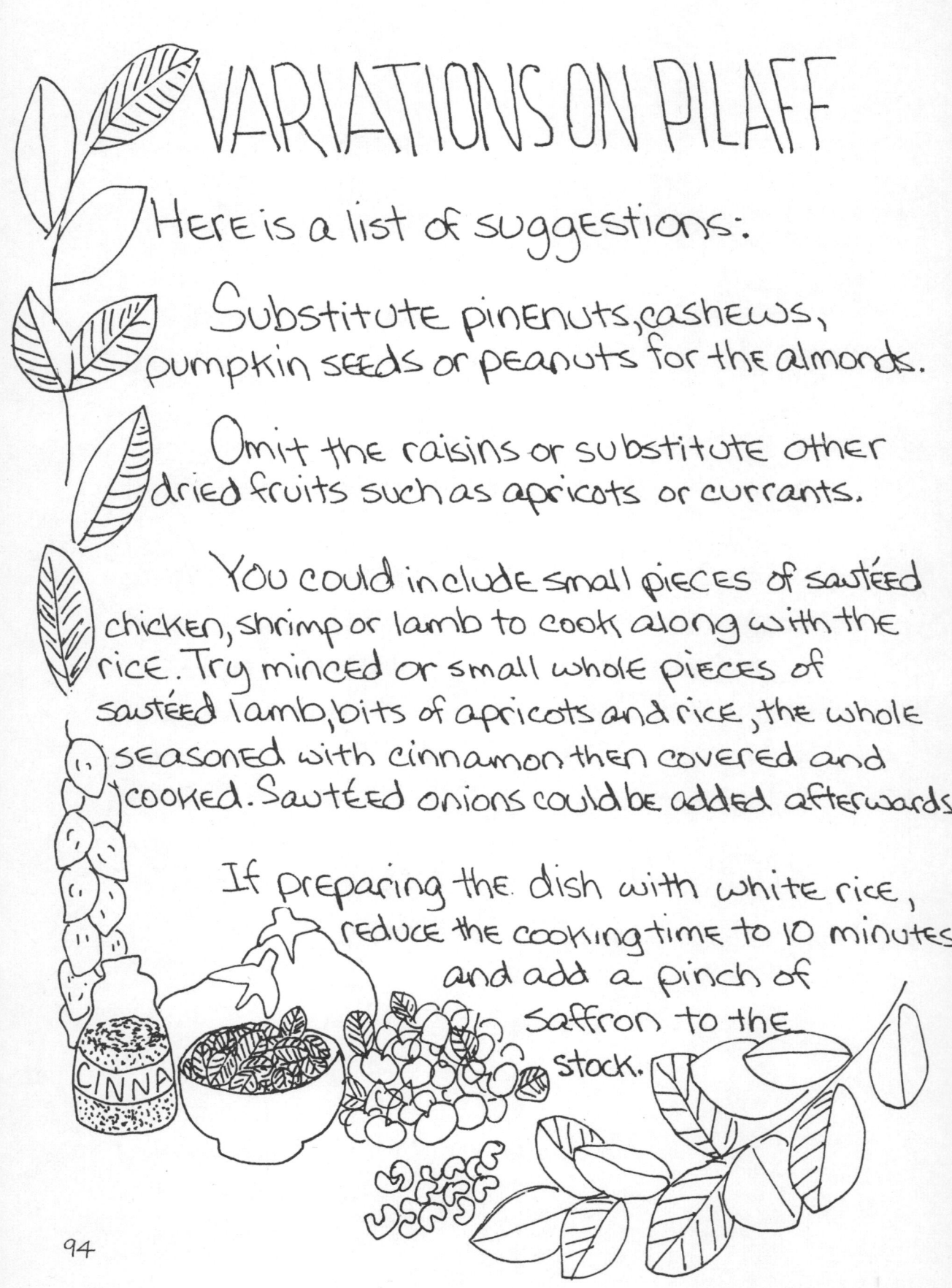

VARIATIONS ON PILAFF

Here is a list of suggestions:

Substitute pinenuts, cashews, pumpkin seeds or peanuts for the almonds.

Omit the raisins or substitute other dried fruits such as apricots or currants.

You could include small pieces of sautéed chicken, shrimp or lamb to cook along with the rice. Try minced or small whole pieces of sautéed lamb, bits of apricots and rice, the whole seasoned with cinnamon then covered and cooked. Sautéed onions could be added afterwards.

If preparing the dish with white rice, reduce the cooking time to 10 minutes and add a pinch of saffron to the stock.

CINNA

A fragrant dish: sauté 1 cup or so of ripe, pitted cherries, adding 1 tbsp. honey and 1 stick cinnamon. Add to this mixture the sautéed rice, chicken stock, 1 tbsp. butter and a pinch saffron. Cover and cook 10-15 minutes.

Or this savory dish: Sauté ½-1 chorizo* sausage, some peas, shrimps, and 1 chopped tomato. Add to the rice, chicken stock and a pinch saffron, then cover and cook 10-15 minutes.

If onions are to be forked into the pilaff, try sautéeing them with a dash of cayenne, cumin, or cinnamon. Vegetables, such as sautéed eggplant strips, cooked pumpkin, peas, lentils or chickpeas, are good this way.

Garnish your pilaff with fresh herbs: sprigs of mint or parsley, coriander leaves. Yogurt is the most refreshing accompaniment as well as spicy harissa (see brik à l'oeuf).

Use your imagination! This dish can be as plain or fancy as you wish.

STUFFED VINE LEAVES (DOLMAS)

Another dish eaten throughout the Middle East, with as many variations as there are cooks.

For the filling:
1 cup raw brown rice or 2 cups cooked brown rice
1 or 2 tbsp. yogurt
2 cloves garlic, crushed
1½-2 tsp. cumin
½-1 tsp. cinnamon

¼ cup raisins
several large sprigs of mint, the leaves removed and chopped
½ onion, chopped

Cook rice, then combine with other ingredients. Other variations to the filling which can be added or substituted according to taste include: ½ lb. minced meat, ¼ cup cooked chickpeas, ¼ cup sautéed pinenuts, 1-2 tbsp. fresh dill or chopped spring onions, or chopped parsley.

For the leaves: Choose brined vine leaves, available in Middle Eastern groceries. Place leaves in a bowl of cold water to soak ½-1 hour, to rid them of excess salt. If using fresh vine leaves, drop into boiling water and blanch 4-5 minutes.

<u>TO STUFF</u>: : Place 1 tbsp. of filling near the bottom of each vine leaf, vein side up and shiny side down. Fold over, first from the bottom, then from the sides, finally rolling up towards the top, like a cigarette. This is much less complicated to do than to explain and after a couple of rolls you will get the feel of it.

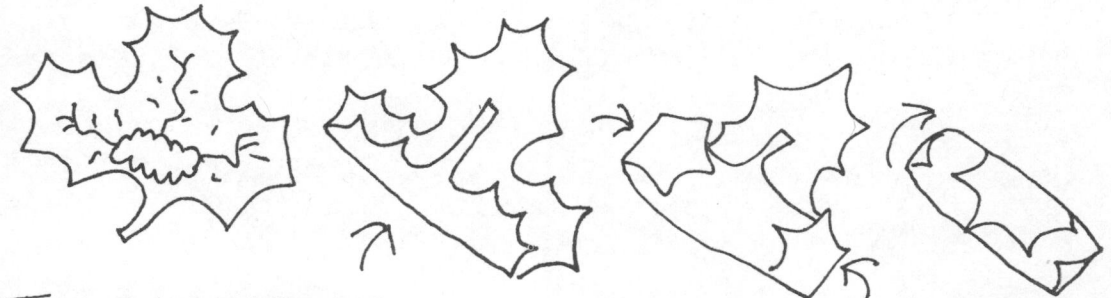

<u>TO COOK</u>: To steam, place in a steamer (a vegetable steamer or a couscousière is perfect) or in a pie pan slightly raised from the bottom of the pot, with boiling water all around.

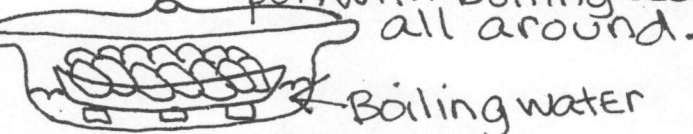

Boiling water

Dribble the juice of ½-1 lemon and ¼ cup olive oil over the parcels before steaming, and tuck in bits of garlic if you wish. Cover and steam 45 minutes, replenishing the boiling water as is needed. Serve hot or cold accompanied by yogurt to dip into or topped with Greek egg lemon sauce.

An alternative method of preparation is to layer the dolmas in a pot with onion slices, 2 tbsp. honey, tomato sauce or fresh tomato slices, cinnamon, lemon juice and salt and pepper to taste. These should be weighted down with a plate or a pie pan to keep them from unrolling, then gently simmered for 45 minutes to 1 hour.

97

KASHA

Kasha*, or buckwheat groats, is a staple in the Russian diet. Cooked plain, it is served with milk and sugar for breakfast or simply added to soups or even bread dough.

This recipe for kasha makes a good accompaniment to pot-roasted chicken, lamb or beef.

Place 2 cups <u>Kasha</u> in a heavy frying pan and toast over a fairly high heat. When roasted brown and fragrant, transfer it to a cooking pot.

Add hot <u>chicken or beef stock</u> to cover, as well as 1 or 2 sliced and sautéed <u>onions</u> and (optional) a handful of <u>mushrooms</u> and 1 <u>sweet green pepper</u>, both sliced and sautéed.

Add 1 or 2 tbsp. <u>nutritional yeast</u>* <u>salt</u> and <u>pepper</u> to taste. Cover, and simmer about 15 minutes, or until the liquid is absorbed.

Toss with <u>butter</u> and serve with gravy from accompanying meat. Serves 6, at least.

FRIJOLES REFRITOS

This Mexican dish can be eaten as it is or in a tostada (a crispy fried tortilla* with beans and salad on top of it) or a taco, (a tortilla rolled around a bit of meat, beans and salad). Literally "refried beans", it is a common accompaniment to almost every main dish served. You can make a large quantity if you wish as the flavor improves over a couple of days.

Place 1 cup pinto beans in a fairly large pot, cover with water and soak overnight (if you haven't time for this step, simply bring the beans to the boil, then soak for an hour or 2). Add several pieces chopped salt pork or streaky bacon, or 1 whole piece bacon rind, several tsp. cumin and a little salt. Bring to the boil.

Reduce heat, cover and simmer 1½–2 hours until beans are tender and there is not much liquid left. If using whole bacon rind, discard now.

Heat a little bacon fat or lard in a frying pan and sauté the beans, ½ cup or so at a time, mashing them with a fork or potato masher as they cook. Mash some and leave others whole. Top with grated cheese and melt before serving. An excellent accompaniment to Huevos Rancheros.

99

CHINESE NOODLE SAUTÉ

Boil 1 lb. chinese style (or any narrow and thin) noodles until just tender; drain and set aside.

Sauté several or all of the following vegetables: 1 or 2 diagonally sliced asparagus spears, 1 diced cucumber, 6 sliced water chestnuts, ½ lb. spinach, 1 chopped spring onion, ¼-½ cup fresh peas. Cook a few minutes, then remove the vegetables from the pan and set them aside.

Sauté ½ lb. minced or shredded pork (or any leftover meat or fowl; duck is excellent) in 1 tsp. peanut or soy oil with 1 chopped spring onion. Mix ¼ cup hoisin, 1-2 tbsp. peanut butter, ½ tsp. white vinegar, and a dash of soy sauce, then add to the sautéed meat. Remove it all from the pan and this, too, is set aside.

Heat several tbsp. of peanut or soy oil in the pan 'til quite hot, then add the noodles and fry 5-8 minutes on a moderate heat. Add the meat and sauce, the vegetables, several lettuce leaves (chopped), a handful of chopped coriander leaves, and a grating of fresh ginger. Toss in 1 cup mung or alfalfa sprouts (see seed sprouts) and 1 grated carrot and dribble 1-2 tbsp. sesame oil * over the whole. Serves 4-6.

A wonderful light meal! Eat with chopsticks and accompany with a light lager.

FISH, POULTRY, and MEAT

SAUTÉED FISH STEAKS

Allow 1 steak per person - <u>halibut</u>, <u>salmon</u>, <u>turbot</u> or whatever else is fresh in the market. Rinse each steak, pat dry, and sprinkle with <u>thyme</u> and chopped <u>parsley</u>

Melt several tbsp. butter in a pan; when foamy add the fish and sauté slowly on both sides. When done (5-7 minutes) remove fish to a hot platter and top each steak with a small pat <u>butter</u> and a squeeze of <u>lemon</u>.

Add ½-¾ cup <u>dry white wine</u> to the pan; raise the heat and cook down the sauce a few minutes. Pour sauce over fish and garnish with parsley, tomatoes and lemon wedges.

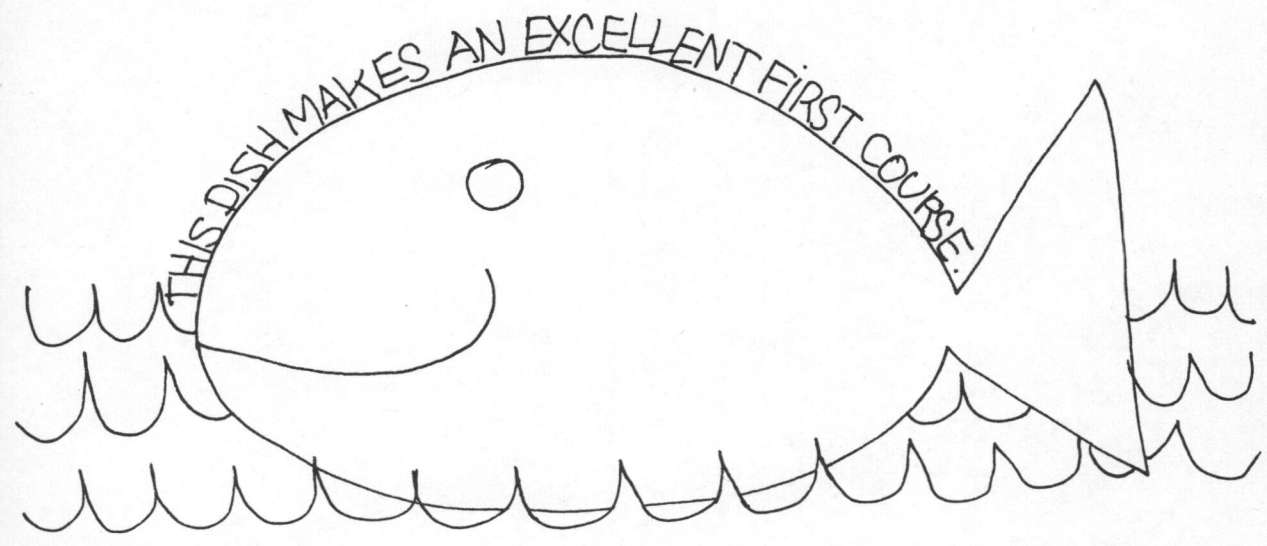

THIS DISH MAKES AN EXCELLENT FIRST COURSE.

COLD POACHED FISH RÉMOULADE

Gently poach 1 <u>fish steak</u> or fillet per person (choose halibut, fillet of sole or any other firm-fleshed white fish) in barely simmering salted water. For each piece allow 5-8 minutes per Lb. (do not overcook!).

Remove the fish steaks using a spatula, taking care not to let them break into pieces. Let cool to room temperature.

Place the cooled fish onto individual <u>lettuce leaves</u> and mask each portion with 2 or 3 tbsp. <u>rémoulade sauce</u>. Decorate with fresh <u>tarragon</u>, <u>watercress</u> and <u>green olives</u>.

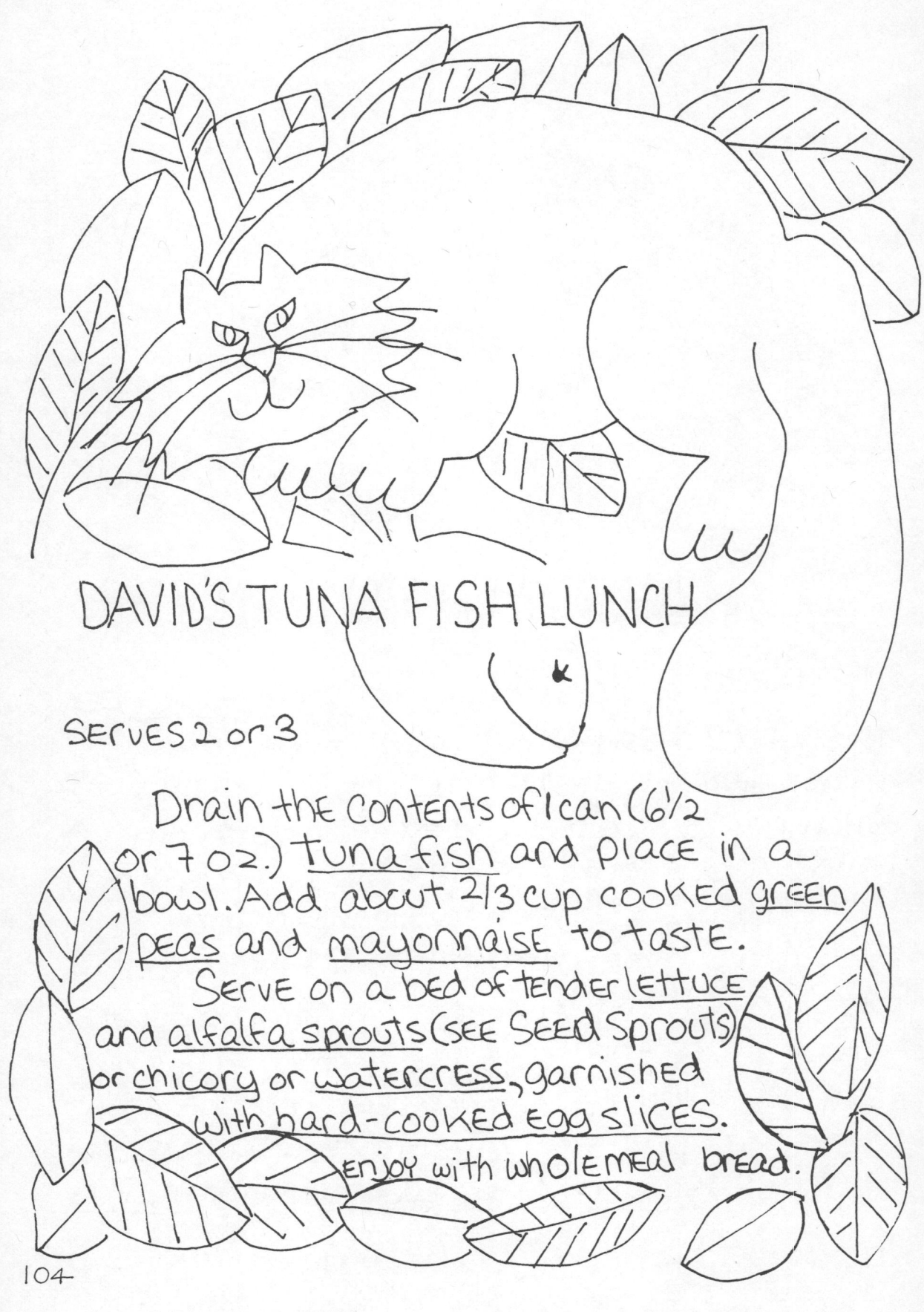

DAVID'S TUNA FISH LUNCH

SERVES 2 or 3

Drain the contents of 1 can (6½ or 7 oz.) tuna fish and place in a bowl. Add about 2/3 cup cooked green peas and mayonnaise to taste.

Serve on a bed of tender lettuce and alfalfa sprouts (see seed sprouts) or chicory or watercress, garnished with hard-cooked egg slices.

Enjoy with wholemeal bread.

ROASTING A CHICKEN
- SOME NOTES -

1. USE a medium oven (300°- 325°, mark 2-3) never letting the heat get high.

2. Stuff the inside with a vegetable. This can be anything fairly mild and fragrant: a wedge or 2 of onion, a stalk of celery, a carrot, several scallions (shallots) or garlic cloves, a slice of marrow, even several lettuce leaves dipped in butter. Whichever vegetable you choose, its function is to keep the bird moist. Instead of dry heat cooking the chicken's cavity, the moist vegetables exude steam which keeps the flesh juicy, while the dry heat of the oven roasts the outer skin nice and crispy.

3. Baste once or twice with chicken drippings, stock or seasoned butter.

4. A sprinkling of paprika before roasting gives the fowl a good hue. Other herbs fond of chicken are tarragon, rosemary, oregano and lemon, garlic, bay leaves and parsley. Perhaps you have your own favorite!

5. For a richer gravy, roast the giblets in the pan alongside the chicken.

The chicken is done when it is golden brown and when its juices run clear and not pink when pricked deeply (about 30 minutes per pound)

ROAST CHICKEN TARRAGON

A succulent dish!

Take 1 whole chicken, minus its head, feet and insides. Rub the outside with a butter mixture (3 tbsp. [1½ oz.] butter creamed with 1 crushed clove garlic, 2 tsp. tarragon, and a grinding of black pepper). Dip several spring onions (if unavailable substitute scallions (shallots) or several small onions and a stalk of celery) into the butter mixture and stuff them into the chicken.

Place chicken in a roasting pan (we use a cast iron frying pan) and roast slowly in a medium oven (about 300°-325°, mark 2-3) for about 2 hours (see notes on 'roasting a chicken). The giblets may be placed in the pan to roast, too. This will enrich the gravy (discard giblets before serving).

When golden brown and fully cooked, heat ¼ cup brandy, cognac, or whiskey. Pour it over the chicken, then ignite! It will burst into beautiful blue flames and the vapors will pleasantly perfume the air. No need to worry, the flames will soon disappear, leaving a subtle fragrant flavor void of alcoholic taste.

Remove chicken to warm plate and place pan on stove. Cook the drippings-liquor-butter sauce down a bit, then stir in ½-⅔ cup cream. Pour gravy over chicken and serve!

CHICKEN PAPRIKASH

2 or 3 <u>onions</u>, chopped
1 or 2 <u>tomatoes</u>,
   PEELED and chopped
1 <u>chicken</u>, jointed
2 cups <u>sour cream</u> or
   very thick yogurt
2 tbsp. rich robust <u>paprika</u>

1 <u>sweet green pepper</u>,
   chopped
1 <u>bay leaf</u>
1 cup <u>white wine</u>
<u>chicken stock</u>
   (several cups)
approx. 3 tbsp. <u>flour</u>
   for thickening sauce

Sauté onions in butter, bacon fat or bland vegetable oil 'til golden. Add the green pepper, tomatoes and paprika and sauté a few minutes longer. Remove mixture and set aside.

Now sauté the chicken pieces, several at a time, sprinkling extra paprika on the pieces as they sauté.

Combine both the chicken and the vegetable mixture in a stewing pot and add the bay leaf. Fill the pot with enough chicken stock to barely cover the chicken, then add the wine. Simmer gently until the chicken is tender, keeping pot covered.

Take 1 cup of liquid from the pot and thicken (with the flour) over the stove (to cook out any taste of raw flour). Return the smooth paste to the rest of the chicken mixture and stir to combine.

Stir in the sour cream, salt and pepper to taste. Excellent over brown rice. Serves 4-5.

CHICKEN LILY

Serves 4

4 boned breasts of chicken
2/3 cup flour seasoned with
    salt, pepper and 1½ tsp. cinnamon
¼ - ⅓ cup chicken stock

Several tbsp. butter
⅓ cup brandy
½ cup cream

Pound each breast gently (this is to tender-ize them slightly and to flatten them enough to brown evenly). Coat each breast with the seasoned flour, shaking off the excess.

Sauté in butter approx. 7 minutes on each side. Be careful not to overcook! When it's golden, it's done. Remove to a warm platter and place in a low oven to stay warm while preparing the sauce.

Add 1 or 2 tbsp. butter to a warm pan, and when that's melted and foamy add 2 tbsp. of flour. Let cook 'til golden, then add stock. Stir and cook a bit then add cream. Continue stirring (with a wooden spoon if possible) 'til smooth. Place chicken in the sauce.

Heat the brandy and when warm pour over chicken. Now, ignite!

Mmm. Serve im-mediately. Accompany with small butter-browned new potatoes, or baked young yams.

PASTILLA (BESTELLA)

An incredibly rich, succulent and unusual dish from Morocco.

SERVES 6

Place 1 small to medium sized chicken (include the gizzards, etc) in a pot, water to cover. Season with 1 large pinch saffron, ½ tsp each ground ginger, cloves and tumeric, 3 cloves garlic, a 3-inch cinnamon stick, ½ cup each coarsely chopped parsley and fresh coriander, and several cubes chicken flavoring, if needed. Simmer for 1-2 hours, until the fowl is meltingly tender.

Strain the stock, reserve the chicken (including gizzards)

and discard any whole spices. Boil the strained stock until it's reduced to 1 cup. Add the juice of 1/2 lemon. Bone the chicken and cut into 1 inch pieces.

Brush the inside of a square or round baking dish approx. 12"x12"x3" with melted butter. Fit a sheet of filo dough (see filo dough pastries) into the dish so that its ends hang over the edge a bit. Brush with melted butter and repeat 5 or 6 times.

Scatter on top of the 6th layer 1/2-2/3 cup of toasted and coarsely chopped almonds. Sprinkle with 1/2 tsp. cinnamon, 1/4 tsp. ground cloves, and 1 tbsp. brown sugar. Beat 4-5 eggs and combine with 1/2 cup stock. Cook slowly until creamy and forming soft curds. Layer 2/3 egg mixture over the almonds and spices. Top with 4-5 more layers of filo dough, buttering each sheet.

Now, arrange the boned chicken pieces and the rest of the egg. Dribble several tbsp. of the remaining stock over this.

Top with another 5-6 sheets buttered filo dough, tucking the overhanging edges from the bottom layers in between. Bake in a 350°-375° (mark 4-5) oven 40 minutes until golden brown. Turn onto a platter and sprinkle with 1 tbsp. cinnamon and 1/3 cup sifted powdered (icing) sugar.

ROSENFELD'S CHINESE DUCK

This recipe makes use of the sort of ceramic pot that is glazed on the inside and in its natural state on the outside. Such a pot should have a tight-fitting lid of the same material. These pots are often made in chicken, fish or other decorative shapes. They give wonderful results with roasted meat, fowl or fish.

Preheat oven to 475° (mark 9). Salt the duck, inside and out, then let sit ½ hour.

Place the duck in ceramic pot, cover and put in oven. Roast approx. 45 minutes, draining off excess fat occasionally.

Remove from oven. Drain off juices and skim off excess fat. Combine the juices with 1 cup of either Chee hou* or Hoisin* sauce. Brush the duck with the juices-sauce mixture and return duck, covered, to the oven for another 30-45 minutes, brushing the duck with the sauce at 15 minute intervals.

Remove from oven. Using a cleaver, chop into bite-size pieces through the bone or else simply remove the meat from the bones. Brush the pieces generously with the sauce and return to the oven to warm through.

Serve with brown rice or steamed bread and chinese-style greens, and garnish with fresh, raw spring onions.

SERVES 4

FONDUE BOURGUIGNONNE

This fondue originated long ago in the vineyards of Burgundy. When the grapes were ripe they had to be harvested immediately; the peasants didn't have time to travel home for the midday meal. Someone had a great idea: a pot of boiling oil in which to cook bits of meat in between working.

2 lb. sirloin or other tender cut of beef
Peanut oil to fill ½ - ⅔ fondue pot
An assortment of sauces

1. Cut meat into 1 inch cubes.
2. Heat oil to bubbling.
3. Each person spears a chunk of meat and cooks it to his taste, then dips it into a sauce.

Serve with fresh French bread, an assortment of sauces and a tossed green salad. Accompany with a hearty burgundy.

SWEET-SOUR SAUCE
Sauté a little chopped onion. Add a dash ginger, several tbsp. tomato sauce, several chunks pineapple and a dash lemon and honey. Cook a few minutes.

TOMATO HERB SAUCE
Sauté a little chopped onion; add garlic, basil, rosemary, parsley, 1 tbsp. red wine, 2-3 tbsp. tomato sauce. Cook several minutes.

OTHER GOOD SAUCES:
Guacamole, Pesto, Dilled Sour cream, Mustard-Mayonnaise Salsa Cruda, Tahina Greek lemon sauce, Baba Ghannouj.

SERVES 6.

We never cease to enjoy this dish!!

LEG OF LAMB, DESERT TRIBE STYLE

Preheat oven to 325, mark 3

With a thin, sharp knife make incisions several inches deep all over the leg of lamb. Do perhaps 10, depending on its size. Into each slit stick a slice of garlic. This will very gently permeate the flesh during cooking.

Now crush a good quantity of garlic, at least 5 cloves. Mix this with a tbsp. or 2 of olive oil and rub this mixture all over the lamb. Shake several tbsp. of ground cumin on to the lamb, coating first the bottom and then the top. This makes a lovely crusty outside and aromatizes the meat during the roasting.

Place in a roasting pan, uncovered, and put it in the warm oven. Roast until crusty and brown outside, to your preferred doneness inside. This is approx. 25-30 minutes per pound, but to eliminate guesswork use a meat thermometer thrust into the thickest part of the meat, not leaning against any bone (150-55° rare, 180° well done).

Serve this excellent lamb with a brown rice pilaff and yogurt. The combination is extremely good.

ROASTED LAMB SHANKS

Place 6 smallish <u>shanks</u> in a baking dish or pan. Sprinkle with 1½ tsp. each of <u>cumin</u> and <u>cinnamon</u>. Add ½ - ⅔ cup <u>raisins</u>, 1 sliced <u>onion</u>, 3 tbsp. <u>honey</u>, 1-2 tbsp. <u>lemon juice</u> and 10 fresh, peeled <u>tomatoes</u> (or a 1 lb. tin tomatoes) plus 1 tbsp. t<u>omato paste</u>. Salt and <u>pepper</u> to taste, and add ½ - 1 cup <u>water</u>.

Bake in a 300° (mark 2) oven, uncovered, 'til tender, approx. 2 hours, turning the heat up to 350° (mark 4) during the last ½ hour. The sauce may be thickened with a little cornflour before serving.

Serve with a pilaff and a yogurt salad
serves 6.

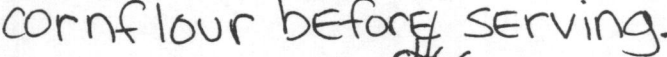

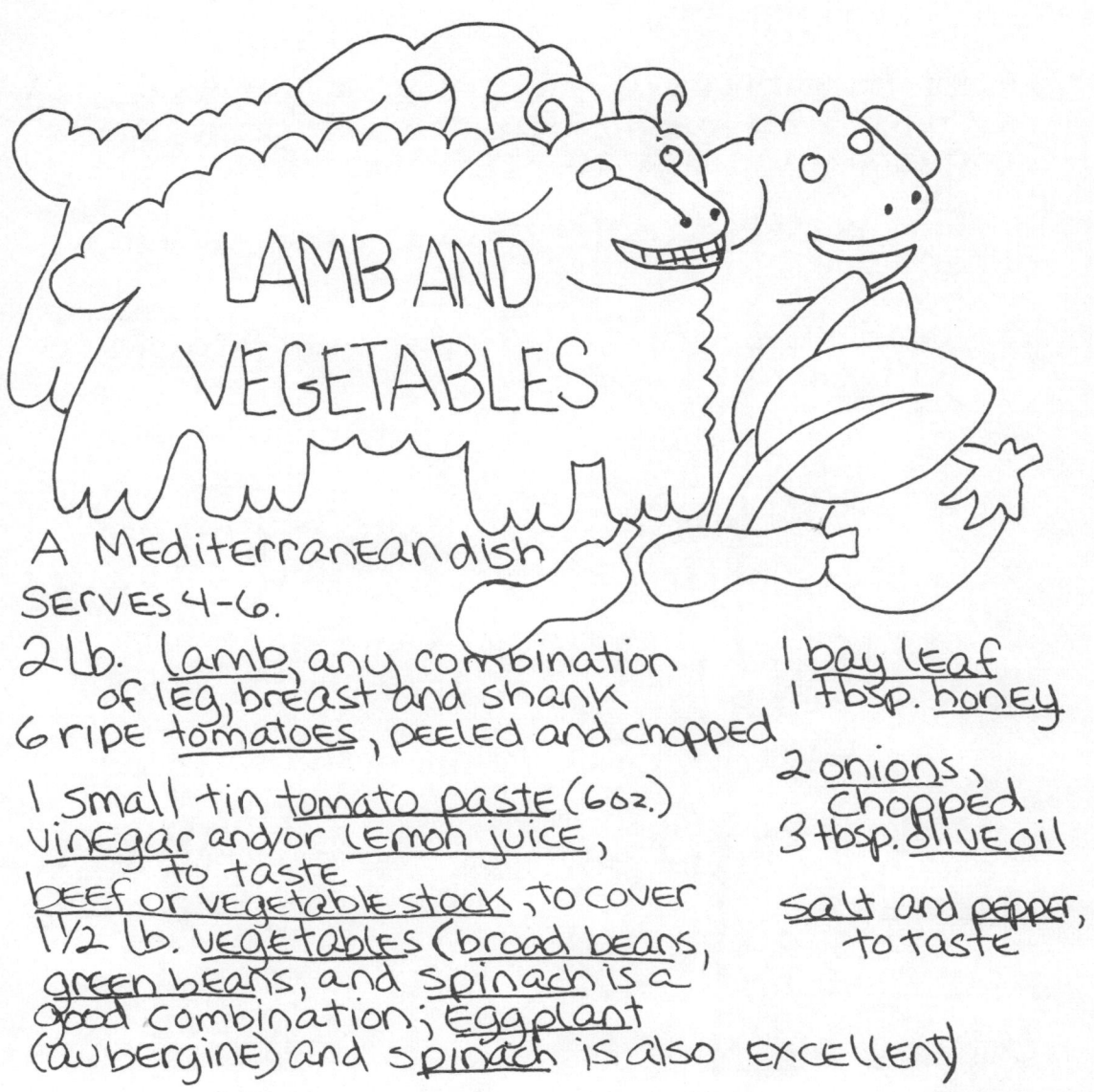

LAMB AND VEGETABLES

A Mediterranean dish

Serves 4-6.

2 lb. lamb, any combination
   of leg, breast and shank
6 ripe tomatoes, peeled and chopped

1 small tin tomato paste (6oz.)
vinegar and/or lemon juice,
   to taste
beef or vegetable stock, to cover
1½ lb. vegetables (broad beans,
green beans, and spinach is a
good combination; eggplant
(aubergine) and spinach is also excellent)

1 bay leaf
1 tbsp. honey

2 onions,
   chopped
3 tbsp. olive oil

salt and pepper,
   to taste

1. Cube the meat and sauté gently in
a little olive oil (together with the shanks
or bony pieces).

2. Add tomatoes, onions, olive oil, the
lemon juice or vinegar, the honey, bay leaf,
half the tomato paste and 1½-2 cups hot
beef or vegetable stock. Simmer gently for an
hour or so (the acid of the vinegar/lemon juice
tenderizes the meat, so if it is not tender enough
add a dash more vinegar or lemon juice
and simmer a while longer).

3. Cube or otherwise cut up the vegetables. Add them and the rest of the tomato paste and simmer until they are tender.

This dish tastes of our first days in Greece.

Serve with brown rice and Arabic yogurt salad.

A STEW OF ROOTS AND LAMB

Flavors of a Rumanian childhood.

9 small parsnips ⎫
7 carrots   ⎬ cut into chunks
2 turnips   ⎭
2 onions, quartered
4 shoulder lamb slices
        or chops
chicken stock to cover

1-2 tsp. paprika
½ tsp. dillweed
(or 1 tbsp. fresh)
Kale, several
leaves, cut up
2 small, new
potatoes, quartered

Place all ingredients in a shallow stewing pot or frying pan with salt and pepper to taste. Bring to the boil, then simmer, covered for 35 - 45 minutes until both meat and vegetables are tender. Pour off ½-1 cup liquid and combine with ⅓ - ½ cup flour. Stir until smooth then return to the stew to thicken gravy and simmer a few minutes to cook out any taste of raw flour.

Pass a bowl of sour cream alongside and accompany the meal with pumpernickel bread.

Serves 4.

MOROCCAN LAMB AND EGGPLANT

Sauté in butter or olive oil 2 thinly sliced onions and 1 clove of garlic until limp, then add 1½ tsp. cumin, ½ - 1 tsp. paprika, ¼ tsp. powdered saffron (or 1 pinch saffron threads), ¼ cup coarsely chopped fresh coriander leaves, a pinch each of ginger and cayenne, and salt and pepper.

Cover 6 small lamb shanks with this mixture, add ½ cup beef broth, 1 or 2 whole cloves of garlic, and a dash of vinegar (to tenderize the meat), then cover and bake in a 325° - 350° oven (mark 3-4) for 1½ - 2 hours until tender.

Meanwhile slice, salt, drain and sauté 1 eggplant (aubergine). Place it in the pan around the lamb, squeeze a little lemon juice into the sauce and bake uncovered ½ hour longer.

Serve garnished with toasted almonds, hard-cooked egg quarters and fresh coriander leaves. Accompany with Moroccan orange salad and crusty bread to scoop up the succulent morsels. Serves 6.

117

MOUSSAKA

A hearty dish, eaten throughout the Balkans and the Middle East. IT is classically prepared with eggplant (aubergine), but when this is not available potato slices are used in its place, and in the early spring tiny zucchini (courgettes) are included. Often on fasting days a meatless moussaka is made, layering the vegetables with tomato sauce and topping with the cheese custard. The Arabs make a moussaka that is a vegetable stew, the main ingredients being eggplant, tomatoes and chickpeas.

This moussaka is Greek, and is well accompanied by a retsina, the Greek resinated wine. The only other dish you need is a simple, green salad, studded with salty black olives and dressed with olive oil, lemon and a sprinkling of oregano.

After such a repast you may wish to dance round the table as in a Greek taverna.

2 eggplants (aubergines)
1 onion, chopped
1 tsp. cinnamon
1 lb. minced lamb
1 chopped and peeled tomato
½ - ¾ cup red wine
1-2 tbsp. tomato paste
½ tsp. oregano
3 tbsp. chopped parsley
2 tbsp. or so wheat germ*
optional: 3 or 4 precooked
   artichoke hearts, sliced

4 tbsp. (2 oz.) butter
2 tbsp. flour
2 cups hot milk
2 whole eggs
1 egg yolk
        slightly
     beaten
1 cup or so mild
   cheese, grated
   (gruyère, parmesan)
pinch grated nutmeg
pinch raw sugar*

Preheat oven to 350° (mark 4).
   Slice the eggplants into ¼-½ inch thick
slices. Sprinkle with salt and let sit half an
hour. Rinse with water and pat dry with a
paper napkin.
   Sauté the dried eggplant slices lightly
in olive oil. Set aside (if using artichoke hearts,
make sure they are already cooked, then simply
sauté and set them aside with the eggplant).

   Sauté the onion 'til golden, then add the
cinnamon and the meat. Stir and sauté. Add
the chopped tomato, wine, tomato paste, oregano,
parsley and the pinch raw sugar. Cook until the
liquid has nearly evaporated and the meat has
lost it's pinkness. Add the wheatgerm, salt and
pepper to taste.
   In a deep casserole dish make a layer
with half the eggplant (and artichoke hearts)
then spread the meat over this. Continue with
another layer of the remaining eggplant. Top
with this custard:
   Melt butter and stir in flour. When flour is
cooked and golden, stir in hot milk. When
sauce is smooth, remove from heat and stir
in eggs and cheese and a pinch of grated nutmeg.
   Pour custard over the top eggplant layer
and bake until the top is golden, 45-50 minutes.
   Serves 4-6.

JAFFA GATE SPINACH
SERVES 4

Season 1 lb. minced lamb with salt, pepper, cumin and ½ chopped onion. Roll into tiny meatballs and sauté lightly.

Soak ⅓-½ cup chickpeas overnight, drain and boil 'til tender (2-3 hours), or use canned chickpeas. Wash 1½ lb. spinach, chop the leaves and stew in butter, covered, until tender (5-7 minutes).

Add spinach, chickpeas and ¼-½ cup chicken stock to meatballs; season with 1 tsp. tumeric, the seeds from 2-4 cardamon pods, salt to taste. Cover and simmer ½ hour.

Sauté 3 crushed garlic cloves in butter with 2 tsp. ground coriander. When fragrant stir in 1-2 tbsp. yogurt. Remove from heat and stir into spinach mixture.

Serve with yogurt and crusty bread.

SAUTÉED LIVER

Slice 4 onions very thinly, then sauté slowly 'til golden, adding salt and pepper to taste and 1½-2 tsp. paprika.

Beat an egg in 1 bowl, place some wheat-germ* in another. TAKE 1 lb. fresh liver, thinly sliced, and dip each slice first in the egg and then in the wheat germ, then sauté in a little butter or oil. Sprinkle with a little paprika and cook 1-3 minutes each side depending on the thickness of the slices

Garnish with minced parsley and serve with the sautéed onions, boiled or steamed spinach and butter-browned new potatoes.

Cold beer or apple juice would go well with this. Serves 4.

SWEETBRREADS ITALIAN STYLE

EVEN if you've no fondness for sweetbreads you'll enjoy this dish.

Sauté several pieces of streaky bacon, (coarsely chopped), 1½ thinly sliced onions and 1 finely chopped carrot for 5 minutes or so.

Add 1 bay leaf, ½ tsp. sweet basil, a sprig of fresh or ½ tsp. dried rosemary, 1½ cups rich beef stock, ¼ cup Madeira wine, 5 peeled and chopped tomatoes (canned ones will do), 2 or 3 crushed garlic cloves, 3 tbsp. chopped parsley, salt and freshly ground pepper to taste.

Bring to the boil, then reduce and simmer, covered, for an hour.

Allow 1 lb. veal sweetbreads for 4 people. Soak in cold water 1 hour; remove excess filaments, connective tissues, etc. Toss into boiling water for about 5 minutes, then remove and plunge sweetbreads into cold water and soak 1 more hour (remove any more excess fibers).

Cut sweetbreads into smallish pieces and combine with the sauce. Cover and bake 35 minutes in a 350° oven, mark 4. Add 10-15 sliced and sautéed mushrooms and return to oven 5 minutes.
To thicken sauce add a little cornflour (cornstarch) mixed with 2-3 tbsp. madeira. Heat together then serve over fresh, firm spaghetti.

CHOUCROUTE GARNIE

A hearty family meal from the French province of Alsace.

Place 5 cups (more or less) sauerkraut in a pot or baking dish. Add 1 bay leaf, 5-6 peppercorns, 4-5 juniper berries, several sprigs of parsley, 1 cup champagne or white wine, 1 cup beef stock, ¼ lb. salt pork or streaky bacon, diced. Simmer or bake in a 250° oven (mark 1) 30-40 minutes.

Prepare an assortment of sausages and smoked meats, allowing perhaps 1 sausage and 1 piece of meat per person, more if the sausages are small or the appetites large. Choose from amongst bockwurst, garlic sausage or any other French or German style sausage available.

Sauté the whole sausages 'til brown and cooked, then put them into the simmering sauerkraut mixture. Continue simmering, while you grill or fry the Kassler (smoked pork chops) ham slices, or any other meat you've chosen.

Presentation: arrange the sauerkraut on a serving platter and garnish with the simmered sausages and the fried meats.

Serve with small boiled or butter-browned potatoes and lots of cold lager.

Serves 6-8.

SAUCES

TAHINA

A creamy sauce made from sesame seeds, tahina is rich, nutritious and favored through-out the Middle East. As a dip it is the consis-tency of a paste or a thick double cream; thin-ned with water it is used as a sauce on fish or vegetables.

Combine: 3 cloves garlic, mashed, 1 tsp. salt, ½ tsp. ground cumin (or more), ¼ – ½ tsp. ground coriander seed, dash cayenne, juice of 2 or 3 lemons, 1 cup sesame paste (canned tahini or see end of recipe for instructions on making your own), ½ cup water.
Add the liquids slowly to the sesame paste to avoid separation. If too thick, add more water, if too thin more sesame paste. Salt and black pepper to taste.

Serve on flat small plates or on one central plate, garnished with olive oil, fresh coriander leaves and a design of sprinkled spices: cumin, tumeric, paprika, cayenne.
Dip into it french or arabic bread.

THE SESAME PASTE:

Sesame paste may be purchased in cans. It is called tahini and is usually found in Middle Eastern food shops (don't buy the Japanese or Chinese for this purpose; it's prepared differently).

If you wish to make it yourself, here are 2 methods to choose from.

1. Place 1 cup sesame seeds, 1/2 cup oil and 3/4 cup or so water in an electric blender. Whirl at a high speed until a creamy sauce develops (if you use this method, decrease the amount of water that you use in making any tahina recipe).

2. Using a flour grinder, grind 1-1/2 cups of sesame seeds. Stir in the 1/2 cup oil.

TWO VARIATIONS:

HUMMUS: Add 1 cup cooked, mashed chickpeas to the prepared tahina sauce. Garnish with olives and pickles and serve as a dip.

BABA GHANNOUJ: Roast 1 whole unpeeled eggplant over a flame (on the top of your stove or over an open fire) until the skin chars and blackens and the inside is soft. Rinse in cold water, and peel off charred skin. This method gives a smoky flavor.

Let eggplant flesh cool and press gently to release its bitter juices; discard the seeds.

Chop finely and mix with 1/2 - 2/3 cup tahina sauce. Garnish with olive oil, parsley, and a sprinkle of cayenne pepper. Enjoy as a dip with bread.

127

GUACAMOLE

Mash 1 or 2 <u>avocados</u>; squeeze a little <u>lemon juice</u> onto the mixture. Add ¼ <u>onion</u>, grated, ¼ <u>tomato</u>, peeled and chopped, and a pinch <u>chilli powder</u> or 1 tsp. <u>salsa cruda</u>. If a fluffier sauce is desired, add 1 or 2 tbsp. <u>mayonnaise</u>. Garnish with fresh <u>coriander</u> and serve with crispy fried tortilla* pieces, or as a sauce with fondue bourguignonne, or in this dish: grate some mild <u>cheese</u> onto a <u>tortilla</u>, add 1 tsp. chopped <u>onion</u> and roll up. Broil (grill) for several minutes to melt the cheese and crisp the tortilla, then serve topped with a spoonful guacamole and a dash of salsa cruda (see following recipe).

Guacamole also makes a good hors d'oeuvre: spread some on a thin slice of bread and top with hard-cooked egg slices, or serve on a bed of shredded lettuce, tomatoes and other fresh salady things and let everyone dip in!

128

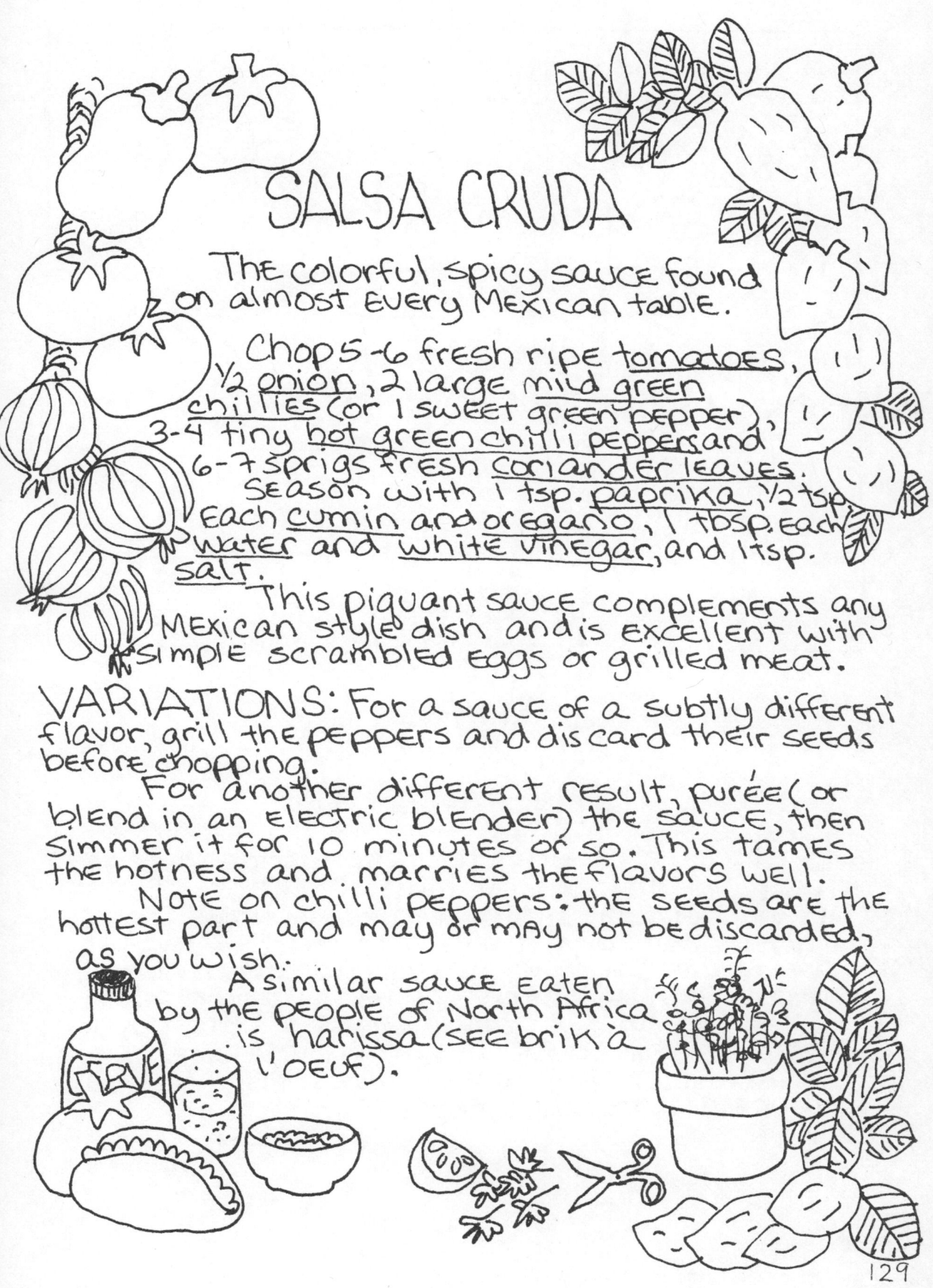

SALSA CRUDA

The colorful, spicy sauce found on almost every Mexican table.

Chop 5-6 fresh ripe <u>tomatoes</u>, ½ <u>onion</u>, 2 large mild <u>green chillies</u> (or 1 sweet green pepper), 3-4 tiny <u>hot green chilli peppers</u> and 6-7 sprigs fresh <u>coriander leaves</u>. Season with 1 tsp. <u>paprika</u>, ½ tsp each <u>cumin</u> and oregano, 1 tbsp. each <u>water</u> and <u>white vinegar</u>, and 1 tsp. <u>salt</u>. This piquant sauce complements any Mexican style dish and is excellent with simple scrambled eggs or grilled meat.

VARIATIONS: For a sauce of a subtly different flavor, grill the peppers and discard their seeds before chopping.

For another different result, purée (or blend in an electric blender) the sauce, then simmer it for 10 minutes or so. This tames the hotness and marries the flavors well.

Note on chilli peppers: the seeds are the hottest part and may or may not be discarded, as you wish.

A similar sauce eaten by the people of North Africa is harissa (see brik à l'oeuf).

PESTO
ALLA
GENOVESE

This is a unique green sauce, a speciality of the Italian city of Genoa. There, in the centuries-old medieval walls where Christopher Columbus spent much of his life, are many small, family restaurants, or trattorias, and each has its very own pesto. Some use lots of garlic, others a little parsley, or a few pinenuts. Its main ingredient is fresh, fragrant basil leaves pounded to a paste and combined with oil!

approx. 2 cups fresh basil leaves

3/4-1 cup grated Parmesan cheese

2-3 cloves of garlic, crushed

1 tsp. salt

1 cup olive oil

Method 1: Crush the basil with a mortar and pestle until it is fairly smooth; then pound, stir and work in the remaining ingredients.

Method 2: Place all ingredients in an electric blender and blend until a coarse purée is formed, turning it on and off so that the thick mixture will not overwork the blender.

Put the purée in a bowl and cover with a film of olive oil.

Variations: ① use half parsley and half basil and/or ② include 1 or 2 tbsp. pine nuts or walnuts or ③ follow the above recipe, but use only ½ the amount of oil, then mash the purée into several tbsp. each of butter and cream cheese.

Serve pesto on ravioli or tortellini, tossed into a salad (1 tsp. mixed with your favorite vinaigrette), floating on top of a minestrone soup, or try this first course: a halved ripe tomato, spread with a tsp. of pesto, topped with a sprinkling of Parmesan cheese and popped under the broiler (grill) for just a moment. Several spoonfuls of pesto is good dribbled over lasagne or cannelloni as an adjunct to the more usual tomato sauce.

Pesto keeps for months in the freezer, though we usually eat it up very quickly!

SATÉ SAUCE

Sauces of this type are popular throughout South-East Asia.

1½ tsp. coriander seed
3/4 tsp. fennel seed   } ground
3/4 tsp. cumin seed
a dash – ¼ tsp. cayenne pepper
1 chopped onion
1 minced garlic clove.
½ cup peanut butter (either buy it or make your own – see nut butters)
1/3 cup meat stock or coconut milk
½ – 1 tsp. brown sugar
juice of ½ lemon

Sauté the onion, garlic and spices for 5 minutes or so. Add the peanut butter, stock and sugar. Simmer 10 minutes and add the lemon juice. Serve with lamb kebabs and rice.

132

MOM'S BARBEQUE SAUCE

Put in a saucepan:

1 tsp. grated onion
1½ tsp. lemon juice
1 cup catsup (ketchup)
⅓ cup worcester sauce
½ tsp. cumin
½ tsp. oregano
1 tsp. salt
¼ tsp. cayenne
2 tbsp. brown sugar
2 tsp. liquid smoke*
or other smoke flavoring
(such as smoky-flavored yeast
or bacon)
2 cups water

Heat it all together gently but do not let it boil. Serve as a sauce for spareribs, hamburgers or any barbequed meat. Try basting meats or chicken with this sauce while they're being grilled.

GREEK LEMON SAUCE

Melt 1 or 2 tbsp. of butter; when foamy, add a tbsp. or so of flour. Stir well, then add 2 cups hot chicken stock; continue to stir so that no lumps form. Set aside.

Beat 2 eggs and add the juice of 1 lemon. Ladle into the egg-lemon mixture some of the chicken stock mixture and stir very well. When it's well combined add another ladle-ful. Stir the egg-lemon-stock mixture into the remaining stock and cook gently, stirring, until sauce thickens. Serve as a sauce for Fondue Bourguignonne or stuffed vine leaves.

133

TOMATO SAUCE

Sauté ½ chopped <u>onion</u> in oil or butter until limp; add 2-3 lb. peeled and chopped <u>tomatoes</u> (canned tomatoes may be used), 1 <u>bay leaf</u>, a pinch of <u>sugar</u> and ½-1 tsp. <u>salt</u>. Simmer 30 minutes to an hour then purée.

<u>Variations</u>: For a thicker, richer sauce simmer longer, for a fresh-tasting lighter sauce, cook only 15–20 minutes. Seasoning with garlic, rosemary, basil and oregano will produce a sauce with an Italian flavor; or season your tomato sauce with cinnamon, cumin and lemon juice and serve with minced lamb for a flavor of the Middle East.

This is a very versatile sauce and can be seasoned to taste or included in other recipes such as paella, or chillies relleños.

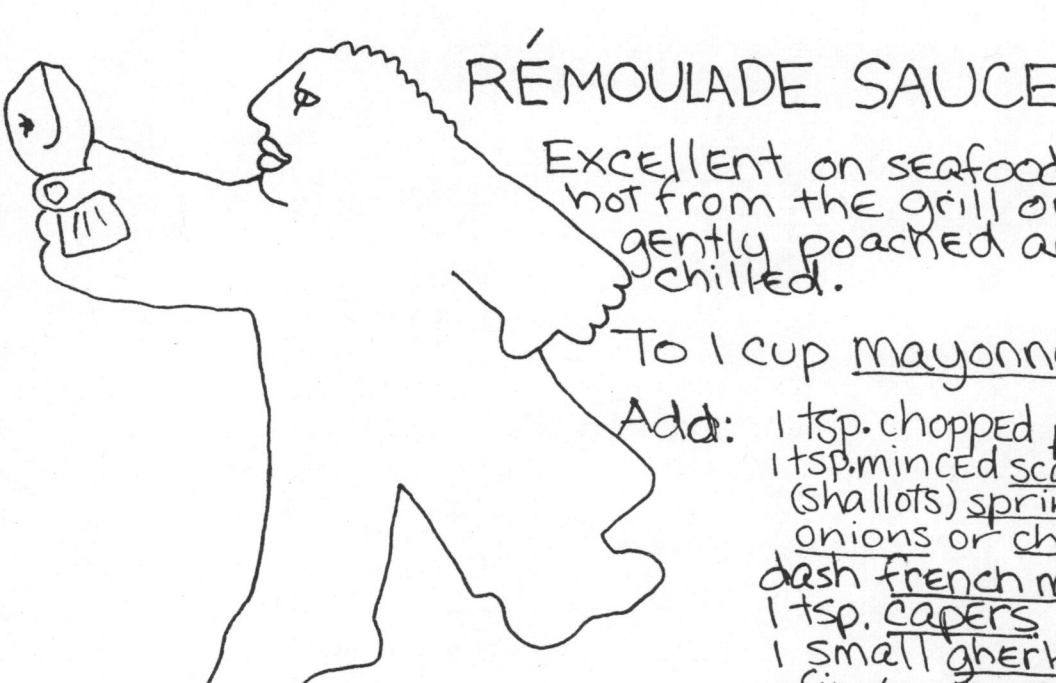

RÉMOULADE SAUCE

Excellent on seafood, hot from the grill or gently poached and chilled.

To 1 cup <u>mayonnaise</u>

Add: 1 tsp. chopped <u>parsley</u>
1 tsp. minced <u>scallions</u> (shallots) <u>spring onions</u> or <u>chives</u>
dash <u>french mustard</u>
1 tsp. <u>capers</u>
1 small <u>gherkin</u>, finely chopped
dash <u>vinegar</u>
½ tsp. <u>Tarragon</u>

OPTIONAL: several sliced pimento-stuffed <u>olives</u> or a mashed <u>egg yolk</u> or ½ tsp. <u>anchovy paste</u> or a little finely chopped <u>cress</u>

Combine all ingredients and chill 'til servingtime.

DILLED SOUR CREAM

1 cup <u>sour cream</u>
½-¾ tsp. <u>powdered bouillon</u>, beef or vegetable
½ <u>onion</u>, thinly sliced
a pinch <u>dillweed</u> (or chopped fresh dill)

Combine and let chill an hour or two. Serve as a dip, using raw carrots, broccoli or cauliflower as "dippers", or spoon some onto a baked potato and top with minced parsley and/or chives. Also excellent as a sauce for fondue bourguignonne.

MUSTARD-MAYONNAISE

To 1 cup <u>mayonnaise</u> add 1 tbsp. mild or french <u>mustard</u> and some thinly sliced or shredded <u>lettuce</u>.

Let sit awhile and use as a sauce with fondue bourguignonne or with a hamburger.

135

SAUCE AU CRÈME

A succulent, creamy, melty sauce.

5 tbsp. (2½ oz.) butter
3/4 cup freshly grated Parmesan cheese

1 crushed clove garlic

1½ cups milk or cream

1 Egg yolk, slightly beaten

½ tsp. basil
a grating of nutmeg

Melt the butter; add the cream or milk. When hot stir in the cheese, garlic and basil. Stir and cook a few minutes more (do not let it boil). Stir in egg yolk and nutmeg and remove from heat.

Toss with the freshly cooked pasta (ravioli, tortellini or any stuffed pasta is best in this sauce).

Enough for 1 lb. stuffed pasta, 4 servings. Accompany with a green salad and perhaps an hors d'oeuvre of melon and prosciutto.

BREADS
and
SANDWICHES

BASIC WHEAT BREAD

1 tbsp. dry yeast
2 tbsp. oil
1/2 cup honey
2 1/2 cups whole wheat flour

1 1/2 tsp. salt
3 cups unbleached white flour

Add the yeast to 1/4 cup lukewarm water and leave until it dissolves and bubbles form, about 10 minutes.

In a large bowl combine the honey, oil, salt, 2 1/4 cups lukewarm water and the dissolved yeast mixture.

Mix in the 3 cups white flour and stir 100 times with a wooden spoon, then mix in the remaining 2 1/2 cups whole wheat flour.

Place the dough on a floured board and knead well with floured hands (to knead: fold the dough in half towards you, then push down on it with the heels of your hands; turn the dough a quarter turn and continue this folding and pushing process until the dough is no longer sticky. Add more flour as needed. The dough is ready when it springs back after being poked).

Oil a large bowl and place dough inside dimpled side down, rubbing the whole dough parcel with oil.

Cover with a clean cloth and let rise in a warm spot (80°-85°F). When doubled in bulk (1½-2 hours) punch down and turn onto the floured board to knead again.

Divide the dough in half and place each in a bread tin (9"x5") or in 1 lb. coffee tins. Allow to rise again 'til doubled in bulk (this time about 45 minutes).

Bake 35-45 minutes in a preheated 350° (mark 4) oven.

VARIATIONS

ONION BREAD

After the first rising knead in 1 sliced and sautéed onion and 2 tsp. fennel seeds. Let rise a second time. Brush with beaten egg over the top and sprinkle with additional sautéed onions and coarse salt. Bake as above.

SOPIAPILLAS

Take the basic bread dough after its first rising. Cut into 2 inch-sided triangle or diamond shapes and flatten each out to ¼ inch. Drop into smoky hot oil, turning once until each side is golden brown. Serve hot, accompanying a spicy meat dish, or as a snack, with butter and honey.

STEAMED BREAD

Begin with the bread dough after the first rising. Cut or break off 2-inch sized pieces and flatten each out. Brush sesame oil* on top of 1 piece and top with another dough piece. Roll out together. Place them in a vegetable steamer or other suitable arrangement. Steam for 10-15 minutes. Where the oil is spread they will separate. Serve hot, with Rosenfeld's Chinese duck.

☆ THE AMERICAN BURGER ☆

Juicy within, still sizzling from the grill; who could resist one?

1½ - 2 lb. minced beef
(include a tiny bit of Heart or kidney)
Several spring onions or scallions (shallots), chopped.

3-4 tbsp. single cream

1 tbsp. wheatgerm*

Gently mix together the above ingredients with your fingers. Shape into 6 patties and sprinkle with salt and pepper to taste. Fry or grill to preferred doneness.

For cheeseburgers, top the nearly cooked patties with a slice of gruyère or cheddar on each, then grill a minute 'til cheese melts.

Serve inside crusty French rolls or sesame seeded "hamburger buns", surrounded by a variety of condiments: mustard-mayonnaise sauce, barbeque sauce, pickles, catsup (ketchup), slices of raw onion, lettuce and tomato.
Accompany with "French fries" (chips) and chilled lager.

140

GUADALAJARA SANDWICH

For each person, take 1 crusty french roll and split in half.

Spread each half with 2 tbsp. refried beans (frijoles refritos). Add several slices cold cooked chicken or beef and top with shredded lettuce, grated cheese and avocado slices. Salt and pepper to taste. Garnish with fresh coriander leaves and use salsa cruda (chilli sauce) and sour cream as condiments.

AVOCADO SANDWICHES

Spread slices of wheat-berry (granary) bread with sweet (unsalted) butter. Add several slices of avocado to each bread slice, and squeeze a dash of lemon juice onto it.

Garnish with minced garlic or spring onion and alfalfa sprouts (see seed sprouts) or shredded lettuce. Salt and pepper to taste.

SWEET
THINGS

LOVERS' FRUIT SALAD

Peel and slice several oranges and place in a bowl with a cup or so of fresh (or, if necessary, frozen) strawberries, halved. Toss with 1-2 tbsp. honey, thinned with a tsp. or water, and ½ tsp. orange flower water.* Let chill ½ hour, then serve, sprinkled with cinnamon.

DANISH FRUIT BOWL

Cut up several cups of fruit, whatever is in season: apples, bananas, berries,
oranges, etc., mixing and matching as
you choose. Add a squeeze of lemon juice
and a dribble of honey. Top with 1 cup
or so thick (double) cream, slightly whipped,
and a grating of chocolate as a fragrant
garnish.

STRAWBERRIES

What more reassuring sign that summer
is coming could there be than the first strawberries of the season.

Do not wash; instead dip each berry into
a little red wine. The wine enhances
their fragrance in a special way.

These wine-rinsed berries need
only be accompanied by a
mound of thick sweet
whipped cream.

145

"TAP-TAP-TAPIOCA
A pleasant pudding.

1. Soak 1 cup large pearl tapioca overnight in 1 cup milk.
2. Next day add 3 more cups milk and simmer slowly for 3 hours.
3. Add 3 whole eggs which have been thinned with a little milk and beaten. Add also several tbsp. mint, chopped (or 2-3 tsp. dried), the seeds from 2-3 cardamon pods, crushed, ½ tsp. almond extract and ¼ cup honey or ⅓ cup brown (raw) sugar*(this can be adjusted to taste).
4. Simmer very lightly a few moments more, then let cool to room temperature, then chill. Best served after a hot and spicy meal. Serves 6-8.

JERUSALEM PASTRY

In old Jerusalem the narrow, cobbled streets are dotted with sweet shops, tiny shops displaying a fantastically wide array of pastries, most of them drenched in a honey syrup.

Surrounding the prospective customer are light fried cakes, crispy baklava-type creations, and nut-filled, honey-soaked rolls. The air is heady with the fragrance of butter, honey and saffron.

Our favorite of these was a pastry always served warm and kept that way on a huge copper tray. The cheese filling is bland and melting, the fragrant syrup delicate as honey straight from the hive.

Reproducing this in our California home, accompanied by thick, strong coffee, we could almost hear the life sounds of the souk in the background.

JERUSALEM PASTRY

1 – 1½ cups <u>couscous</u>*
½ – ⅔ cup (¼–⅓ lb) <u>butter</u>
1 lb. <u>ricotta cheese</u>*
1 beaten <u>egg</u>
a pinch of <u>salt</u>

2 tbsp. <u>honey</u>
pinch cinnamon
¼ – ½ cup semi-
soft bland cheese.
(<u>muenster</u>* or
<u>monterey Jack</u>*)

Steam the couscous in a couscousière or a colander placed over boiling water for 30-40 minutes. Rub between your hands to dissolve any lumps, then combine it with the butter and simmer a few minutes until the butter is absorbed. Add a pinch of salt and 1 beaten egg, stirring to combine.

Spread half the mixture on the bottom of a 9×9 inch pan. Pat down as firmly as possible. Spread this with a mixture of the cheese, honey and cinnamon, well combined, and top with a layer of the remaining couscous, pressing gently.

Bake in a pre-heated 400° oven (mark 6) 10-15 minutes. Then place under broiler (grill) a few minutes to get a crisper golden brown crust.

Meanwhile, make a syrup with 1¼ cups <u>honey</u>, ½ cup <u>water</u>, ¼ tsp. or a little more <u>saffron</u> and 1 tsp. either <u>orange flower water</u>* or <u>lemon juice</u>. Bring to the boil and continue boiling 5-7 minutes.

Using a ladle, gently bathe the pastry in the syrup, letting it drip down softly so as not to disturb the crust.

Let stand ½ hour or until the pastry has absorbed the syrup. Serve cut into squares.

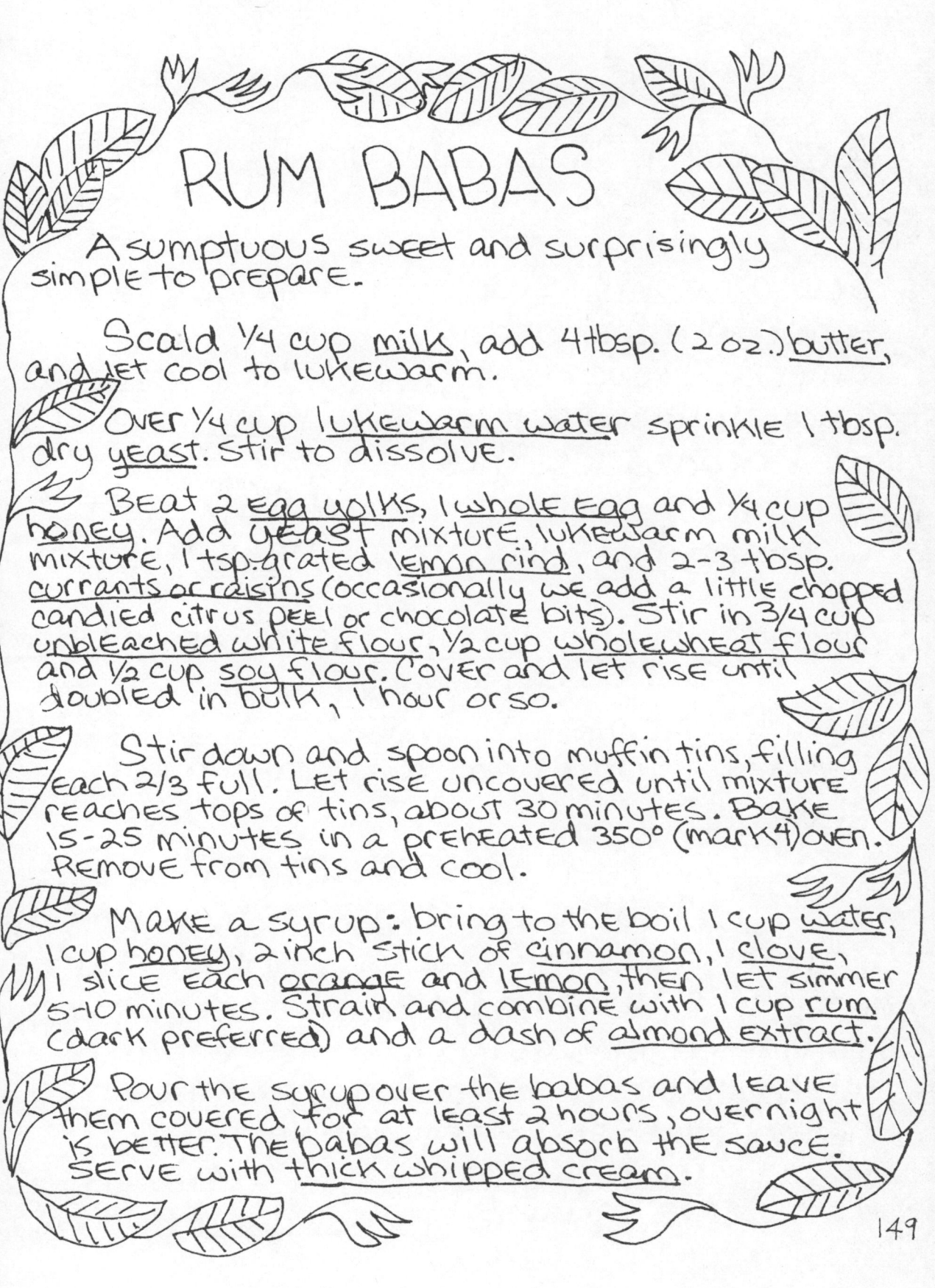

RUM BABAS

A sumptuous sweet and surprisingly simple to prepare.

Scald ¼ cup <u>milk</u>, add 4 tbsp. (2 oz.) <u>butter</u>, and let cool to lukewarm.

Over ¼ cup <u>lukewarm water</u> sprinkle 1 tbsp. dry <u>yeast</u>. Stir to dissolve.

Beat 2 <u>egg yolks</u>, 1 <u>whole egg</u> and ¼ cup <u>honey</u>. Add <u>yeast</u> mixture, lukewarm milk mixture, 1 tsp. grated <u>lemon rind</u>, and 2-3 tbsp. <u>currants or raisins</u> (occasionally we add a little chopped candied citrus peel or chocolate bits). Stir in ¾ cup <u>unbleached white flour</u>, ½ cup <u>wholewheat flour</u> and ½ cup <u>soy flour</u>. Cover and let rise until doubled in bulk, 1 hour or so.

Stir down and spoon into muffin tins, filling each 2/3 full. Let rise uncovered until mixture reaches tops of tins, about 30 minutes. Bake 15-25 minutes in a preheated 350° (mark 4) oven. Remove from tins and cool.

Make a syrup: bring to the boil 1 cup <u>water</u>, 1 cup <u>honey</u>, 2 inch stick of <u>cinnamon</u>, 1 <u>clove</u>, 1 slice each <u>orange</u> and <u>lemon</u>, then let simmer 5-10 minutes. Strain and combine with 1 cup <u>rum</u> (dark preferred) and a dash of <u>almond extract</u>.

Pour the syrup over the babas and leave them covered for at least 2 hours, overnight is better. The babas will absorb the sauce. Serve with <u>thick whipped cream</u>.

ALMOND PASTRIES

8 oz. almond paste (or substitute 8 oz. ground almonds, 1/3 cup honey, a dash almond extract, all kneaded together)

1 or 2 tbsp. honey or sugar

approx. 1/4 lb. filo dough (see filo dough pastries)

1 Egg

3 tbsp. orange flower water*

4 tbsp. sweet (unsalted) butter

dash almond extract

Combine all ingredients (except filo dough) and beat to a smooth consistency.

Turn oven to 350°-375° (mark 4-5).

Lay out 1 sheet of filo dough; brush with melted butter and lay another sheet on top of it. Along 1 edge of the sheets, place a roll of the almond mixture. Fold both side edges over an inch or so toward the center, then roll up to enclose the filling.

Bake until golden brown (about 10 minutes). Serve sprinkled with sugar and cinnamon.

POPPY SEED STRUDEL

Poppy seeds make us feel very alive. Do they do that to you, also?

2 cups poppy seeds freshly ground in a grinder or an electric blender

1/3 cup raisins, chopped

1/4 package or 1/4 lb. filo dough (see filo dough pastries)

1/2 cup honey
1/2 cup milk
grated rind of 1/2 lemon.

Cook everything but the filo dough over a very low heat 5-7 minutes. Leave to cool.

Lay out several layers of filo dough on top of one another, brushed in between with melted sweet (unsalted) butter. Place 1/2 the filling lengthwise along 1 edge of the dough sheets. Roll up, enclosing the filling in the center, and folding to seal up the ends.

Repeat with the rest of the filling and dough sheets.

Bake in a 400° (mark 6) oven 10-15 minutes until golden brown. Serve cold, cut into pieces.

MISCELLANY

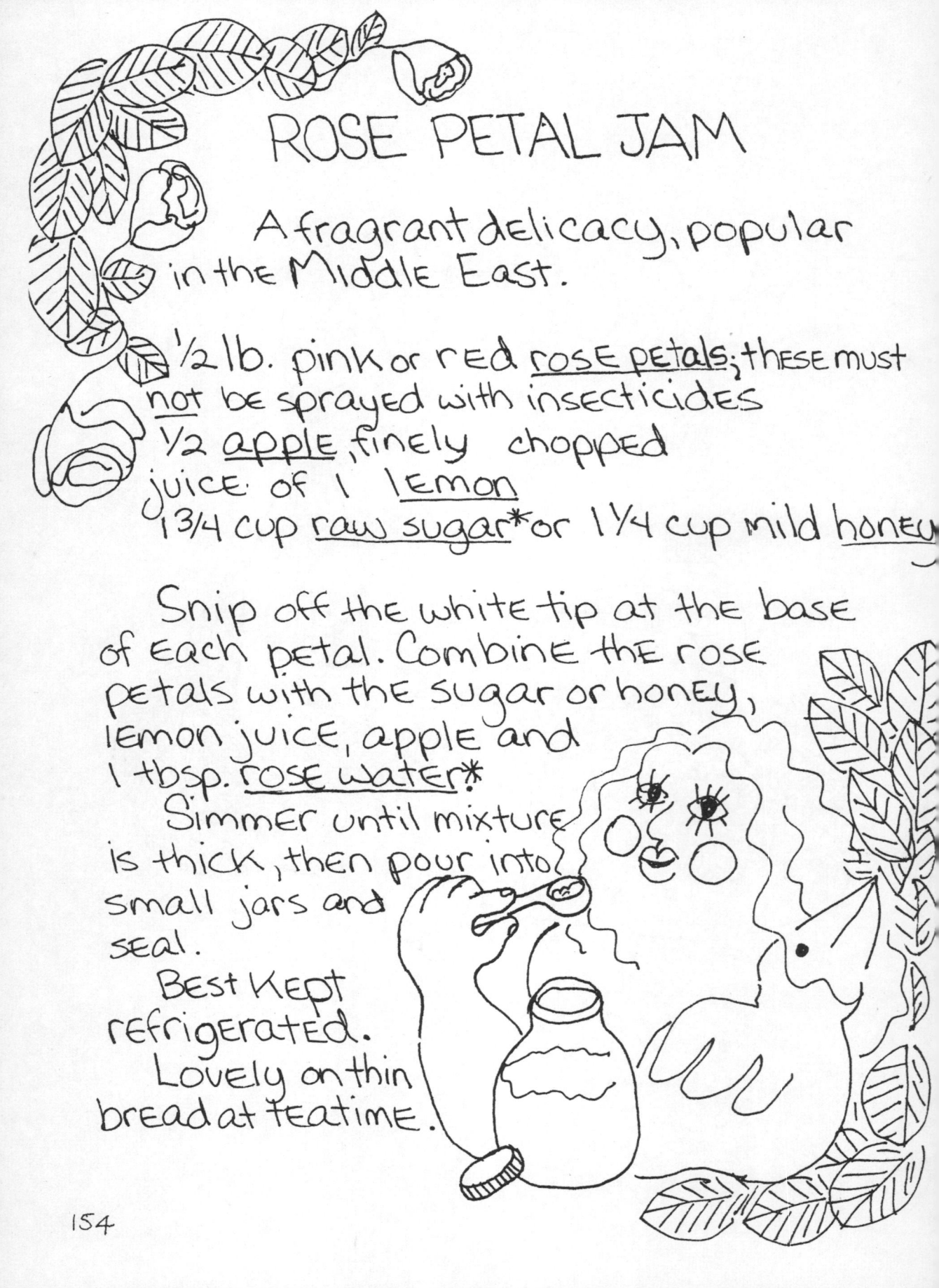

ROSE PETAL JAM

A fragrant delicacy, popular in the Middle East.

½ lb. pink or red <u>rose petals</u>; these must <u>not</u> be sprayed with insecticides
½ <u>apple</u>, finely chopped
juice of 1 <u>lemon</u>
1 3/4 cup <u>raw sugar</u>* or 1 1/4 cup mild <u>honey</u>

Snip off the white tip at the base of each petal. Combine the rose petals with the sugar or honey, lemon juice, apple and 1 tbsp. <u>rose water</u>*

Simmer until mixture is thick, then pour into small jars and seal.

Best kept refrigerated.

Lovely on thin bread at teatime.

NUT BUTTERS

A tasty, nutritious spread, delicious on bread or as a basis for many sauces, most notably those eaten with the satés (kebabs) and gado-gado (a vegetable dish) of Indonesia.

Using an electric blender: whirl 1 cup nuts in a blender until finely ground, then add a little oil (2 tbsp.-1/4 cup of peanut or soy oil) 'til it reaches the consistency preferred. This mixture is quite thick, so turn on and off, taking care not to overtax the blender. Salt to taste.

Using a grinder: grind the nuts in the grinder, then combine with the oil, stir well, and salt to taste.

(Choose peanuts, almonds, cashews or whatever nuts you prefer. Use them raw or toasted.) Delicious spread on whole-meal bread and dribbled with honey.

BREAD AND BUTTER PICKLES

This is our version of an American favorite. No one seems to know where the name came from (though it does make a tasty snack with bread and butter).

A good pickle to make if you have a garden and have an abundance of the vegetables; anyhow, you will be pleased with its sweet, spicy and sour flavor.

approx. 4 lb. sliced zucchini, cucumber or summer squash
6 sliced onions
2 chopped sweet green peppers
3 cloves garlic
1/3 cup coarse salt

5 cups brown sugar
2 tsp. tumeric
2 tsp. celery seed
2½ tbsp. mustard
3 cups cider vinegar

Combine sliced zucchini, onions, peppers and whole garlic cloves. Add salt; cover with coarsely broken ice and mix thoroughly. Let stand 3 hours; drain.

Combine remaining ingredients and pour over vegetable mixture. Heat all just to boiling point. Seal in hot sterilized jars.

This is especially good enjoyed with tuna fish salad and bread or with hamburgers.

SEED SPROUTS

Sprouts are tasty, nutritious and extremely inexpensive if you make them yourself.

Choose any <u>untreated</u> (with insecticides) <u>seeds</u>: <u>soy bean</u>, <u>mung dhal</u>, <u>lentil</u>, <u>cress</u>, <u>whole wheat kernels</u>, <u>fenugreek</u> or <u>alfalfa</u>, our favorite.

Place several tbsp. of the seeds in the bottom of a wide-topped jar, fill jar with water and let seeds soak 2 hours.

Drain and place in a cupboard or other dark place. Cover jar with a piece of cloth to protect against dust, insects, etc.

Rinse and drain twice a day; within 3-5 days your sprouts should be ready for eating.

Enjoy raw, in salads or sandwiches, or sauté some onion and sweet pepper with mung bean sprouts and a seasoning of soy sauce.

YOGURT

A wonderful solid milk food with a refreshing, slightly tart taste, yogurt is eaten throughout the Middle East, the Balkans, India, Afghanistan and Armenia. It is abundant in B vitamins and many people claim that eating it ensures a long, healthy life.

Yogurt may be made in the home very easily. Simply heat 4 cups milk (whole milk for a richer yogurt, skimmed milk for a lighter low-fat result) to a temperature of 180°, or until bubbles form round the edge. Let it cool to lukewarm or until the milk is just warmer than your wrist.

Pour milk into a jar or ceramic bowl and stir in 1/4 cup live yogurt (use your favorite unflavored type; we recommend a Greek or Armenian yogurt). Cover with a well-fitting lid, wrap in a towel, and put in a warm, draft-free spot for 6 hours or overnight.

Transfer to the refrigerator to chill a few hours and to solidify a bit.

Enjoy as a sauce, salad or marinade, or as a snack with fruit, honey and wheatgerm*

FILO DOUGH PASTRIES

Have you ever eaten baklava and marvelled at the paper-thin pastry, crispy golden and delicate?

The name of the dough is filo (phyllo, fila - there are several other ways of spelling it) and it's the basis of many different pastries throughout the Middle East. IT is easiest to buy it in packets at Greek or international groceries. When handling this dough be careful of the tissue-like pastry sheets - we once threw away half a packet thinking it was still the paper wrapping.

If you wish to make your own, here is a recipe from the Home Book of Greek Cookery by Joyce Stubbs:

12 oz. [3 cups] flour   pinch of salt
1 dessertspoon olive oil   water

Sift the flour and salt together, add the oil and as much water as is required to make a firm dough. Knead well and roll out as thinly as possible on a floured cloth, and with the hands stretch gently and carefully until the dough is stretched to the thinness of paper. Leave to dry for 3/4 hour and use as is required.

These are the 2 basic ways of handling filo dough:

1. Brush the individual sheets with melted butter, wrap them each around a filling, then bake.

2. Use no fat while wrapping the filling but deep-fry the pastry instead of baking it. Pastries cooked in this way are popular in North Africa.

The variety of these pastries is almost unlimited. They can be tiny hors d'oeuvre size, or larger but still individual pastries, or large pies able to feed a dozen people. They can be sweet and layered with nuts or custard or savory and/or spicy.

One of the most standard pastry shapes is the triangle:

It is a good idea to practise folding this with paper first.

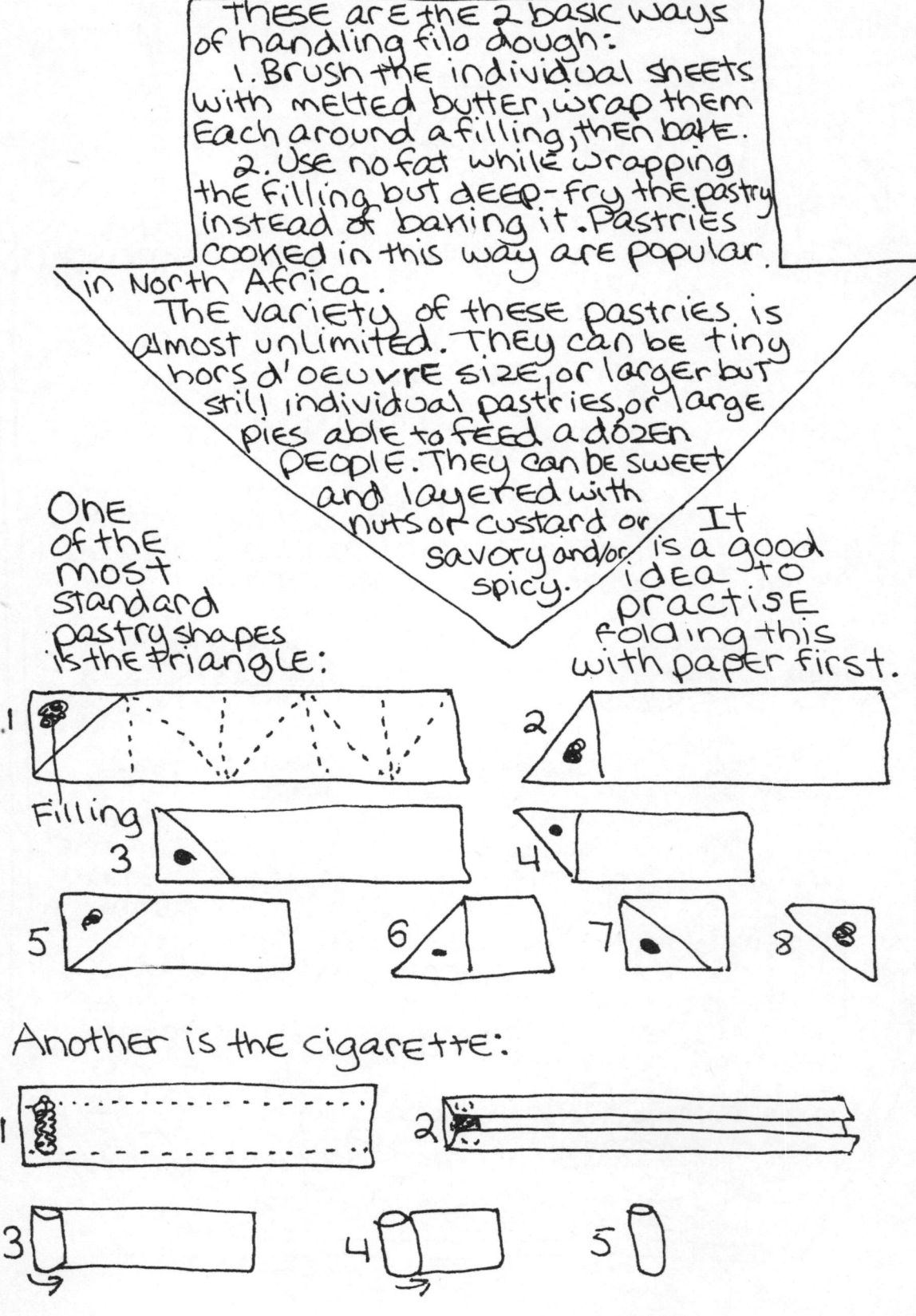

Filling

Another is the cigarette:

FRAGRANT
HERBED VINEGAR

Herbed vinegar is simple to make, a nice gift for friends and a good reason for saving those old wine bottles.

Into the bottom of each bottle place any combination of the following: several cloves _garlic_, 1/2 tsp. _basil_, 1 tsp. whole _peppercorns_, sprig of _rosemary_, _tarragon_, _thyme_, _oregano_, _mint_ or _mustard seeds_. Garlic and tarragon are especially good together.

Fill the bottles with a half and half mixture of _red wine vinegar_ and _white clear distilled vinegar_. Cork the bottles and leave to sit in a sunny window for several weeks. This will keep indefinitely — in fact, it improves with age.

Another idea is to save leftover bits of _wine_ and add it to the vinegar.

SUPERB!

VIN

TURKISH COFFEE

A favorite also among the Greeks and Arabs.

The utensil used for boiling Turkish coffee is the small pot pictured below.

For each person, into the coffee pot place 1 tsp. Turkish ground coffee (so fine as to be almost a powder), 1 tsp. sugar (more or less according to taste), several seeds or 1 whole pod of cardamon, and a tiny Turkish coffee cupful water.

Place on a high heat and bring to the boil. Remove from heat and repeat the process until the coffee has boiled 3 times.

Serve in tiny cups and accompany with sweets.

INDEX